Hold your Water!

68 Things You Need to Know to Keep Our Planet Blue

Wyland

With Steve Creech and Sue Ann Balogh

Foreword by Spencer Johnson, M.D.

Andrews McMeel
Publishing, LLC
Kansas City

06 07 08 09 10 RR2 10 9 8 7 6 5 4 3 2 1

ISBN-13: 978-0-7407-5682-5
ISBN-10: 0-7407-5682-6

Library of Congress Cataloging-in-Publication Data
Hold your water : 68 things you need to know to keep our planet blue / by The Wyland Foundation
    with Steve Creech and Sue Ann Balogh.
        p. cm.
    ISBN 0-7407-5682-6
    1. Water conservation. 2. Water supply. 3. Water quality. I. Creech, Steve. II. Balogh, Sue Ann.
III. Wyland Foundation.
    TD388.H65 2006
    333.91'16—dc22

2005058907

www.andrewsmcmeel.com

Book design by Holly Camerlinck

Attention: Schools and Businesses
Andrews McMeel books are available at quantity discounts with bulk purchase for educational, business, or sales promotional use. For information, please write to: Special Sales Department, Andrews McMeel Publishing, LLC, 4520 Main Street, Kansas City, Missouri 64111.

For Rachel Carson, who knew that hope for our
planet lay with the very human qualities of reason, courage,
and compassion. And for Dr. Sylvia Earle,
a scientific and environmental pioneer in her own right.
And, perhaps most off all, for all those who are "making waves"
to keep our planet blue for generations to come.

Contents

Foreword ix

Preface. xi

Acknowledgments xiii

Introduction xv

Part I
Getting Your Feet Wet . . . 1

1	It's So Big.	2
2	It's So Wet	4
3	Now That I'm on the Water Cycle, How Do I Get Off?	6
4	Even the Trees Are in on It	8
5	What Is a Dead Zone, Anyway?	10
6	Only Chumps Dump.	12
7	Shower Power.	14
8	The Car Wash Blues.	16
9	The Inside Poop on Pet Waste	18
10	How Does Your Garden Grow?.	20
11	Wanted: More Graffiti	22
12	Jellies on a Roll	24
13	Bottle Bashing	26
14	If You Love It, Set It Free.	28
15	The Great Weight Debate	30
16	Start a "Pee Outside" Day	32

17   A Cure for Buildup 34

18   Beat the Wrap 36

Part 2
What Are You Calling a Bad Habit? . . . 39

19   Hold on to Your Butt. 40

20   Beware of Things That Go Drip in the Night 42

21   Fish Don't Get Depressed, So Why Are We Giving Them Prozac? 44

22   Seconds Anyone?. 46

23   Water Color: The Politics of Conservation 48

24   Try Green Cleaning. 50

25   Colonel Halibut in the Library with a Fishing Pole 54

26   I'm Melting in the Rain. 56

27   How the Other Half Lives 58

28   Letting Creativity Flow 60

29   Whose Water Is It, Anyway?. 62

30   A Thirstier World. 64

31   Shouldn't I Know Something About the Greenhouse Effect? 66

32   Grab Bag 68

33   Small Car, Big Savings 70

34   Fishometers 72

35   Breeding Goodwill 74

Part 3
Go with the Flow . . . 77

36   Welcome to Disposable Island 78

37   A Stranger in Your Tank 80

38   Make Your House a Home. 82

39   Smart Dinner Talk 84

40   Watered-Down Techno Trash. 87

41 The Trouble with MTBE 90
42 Hooked on Dry-Cleaning 92
43 Wild, Wonderful Wetlands 96
44 Power of the Pen. 98
45 Watchdog for Water 100

Part 4
A Global View ... 103

46 Unsafe Water: The Human Cost. 104
47 A Head Start on Innovation 106
48 People, People Everywhere—and Only So Many Drops to Drink. 108
49 Vanishing Act 110
50 Where's Your Next Drink Coming From? 112
51 Are You Retaining Enough Water? 114
52 A Big Dip in the Great Lakes 117
53 Debt for Nature 119
54 Buy More! Save Less? 122
55 Drops for Crops 126
56 Sharing Scenarios 128
57 Big Blue Battery 130
58 Winds of Climate Change 132
59 What's in a Name? 134
60 A Tip About Aquaculture 136
61 Trawling for Dollars 138
62 A Dry Look at Toilets 140

Part 5
Strange Weather Ahead ... 143

63 Negative Flow 144
64 View from the Greenhouse 146

65 Desert by Numbers 148

66 Making a Stink About Methane 150

67 Express Yourself 153

68 Holding Back a Flood 155

Appendixes . . . 159

Appendix 1 Quick Tips for Water Conservation in the Home. 159

Appendix 2 Quick Tips for Smart Seafood Dining 161

Appendix 3 Pathogens—When Good Water Goes Bad 162

Appendix 4 A Look At Your Water Bill. 163

Appendix 5 Solving the Water Crisis? 165

Appendix 6 Sample Advocacy Letters 165

Appendix 7 Getting to Know the Clean Water Act 168

Appendix 8 Fifty Environmental Organizations Worth Supporting. 169

Appendix 9 Start Now: Water By the Numbers 170

Glossary 171

Resources 175

About the Wyland Foundation 182

About the Authors. 183

Foreword

Wyland's Changing World of Water

Water and Wyland go together. And we can all benefit from it!

Water is the most precious life-supporting resource we have. And Wyland, the world's leading marine artist, has a passion for restoring pure water to the earth that is unparalleled.

You may remember when an abundance of pure drinking water flowed from our faucets at home, and it was practically free.

A lot about water has changed. Like most changes, it happened a little bit at a time. As you will read, many people did a few thoughtless little things that didn't seem to matter. But they added up and reduced the purity of our cities' water supplies and thus reduced the quality of the water we drink.

Not that many years ago, very few of us thought we would ever go to the market and pay good money for bottles of drinking water. Yet it is happening.

Now, in Wyland's wonderful book, you can discover not only how water has changed, but how *you* can change, and help us regain our clear water.

In the "Tips" sections of the book, you will see how each of us can easily do some *little* things differently in our own lives—things that will add up and make a *big* difference to our regaining a clean water supply.

Hold Your Water may be a strange title for a book, but the content is terrific. Then again, who am I to talk about unusual book titles?

—Spencer Johnson, M.D.,
Author, *Who Moved My Cheese?:
An A-Mazing Way to Deal with Change*

It is our task in our time and in our generation, to hand down undiminished to those who come after us, as was handed down to us by those who went before, the natural wealth and beauty which is ours.

—JOHN F. KENNEDY

Clean water and healthy oceans will be one of the most important issues of the next century.

—WYLAND

Every man, woman, and child is a small river . . . 70 percent of our bodies is water. A 1 percent deficiency of water in our body makes us thirsty, 5 percent causes a slight fever, and at 10 percent we become immobile. A 12 percent loss of water and we die.

—PETER SWANSON, *Water: The Drop of Life,* 2001

Preface

How do you make a difference? How do you leave a legacy of a healthy environment for future generations? What if you realized that you could change the world by changing a habit here or there? What if you read a newspaper and suddenly realized that two seemingly different issues, say, the kind of household cleaners you use and the health of a local stream, were very closely linked together? The fact is *you don't need to be an activist or a scientist to make a difference.* Right now, the future of our planet needs everybody: teachers, engineers, doctors, administrators, accountants, biologists, mechanics, students, athletes, artists, writers, lawyers, and fishermen. No one is excluded. They can't be. Why? Because people from all walks of life will shape the world of tomorrow. The decisions each of us makes today will change the face of the planet in twenty years.

Hold Your Water! 68 Things You Need to Know to Keep Our Planet Blue was written for people like you. It's a quick—and fascinating—look at the many different ways human activity impacts the health of water around the world. We explore the latest news, technologies, and facts about our world of water, but most important, we try to provide answers and solutions. Some of these might be as simple as cleaning up pet waste or reducing your carbon footprint (don't worry, we'll explain more about that later). Other solutions include tips on making your voice heard by lawmakers and other decision makers.

I've spent my life creating monumental works of art to raise awareness about the beauty and importance of marine life habitats. I've met with leaders around the world who are concerned about the health of our oceans, lakes, streams, and wetlands. And I've worked with people behind the scenes—the ones who get things done. These are extraordinary people doing extraordinary work. But what amazes me most about many of these people is that they are constantly learning and striving for a better understanding of our environment and how we can live in harmony with our planet.

That is what we hope to accomplish with this book. You can read a page here or a page there. You can start at the back and work your way to the front. There is no right or wrong way. If you're a person who wants to make changes right now, we've added appendixes with dozens of tips, so you can find new ways that you can change habits at home. The good news is that you, as an educated consumer, have the power to change things for the better. Your kids do, too. If it starts with this book, all the better. Hopefully, if you're like me, you'll discover the connections that lead to one of those aha! moments. Once that happens, you're on your way.

—Wyland

Acknowledgments

The Wyland Foundation has discovered that there is a widespread lack of knowledge about the delicate and intricate nature of ecosystems and the connection between what we do as humans and the impact on our oceans, lakes, rivers, streams, ponds, and wetlands. The Ocean Project's National Survey (1999) found that when asked to choose the main source of ocean pollution among three sources, only 14 percent of Americans selected the correct answer—runoff from yards, pavement, and farms. The same survey also showed that 45 percent of Americans agreed with the statement "What I do in my life doesn't impact ocean health much at all."

Since 1993, the Wyland Foundation has addressed these issues by creating memorable and educational art and science experiences for people of all ages that have lasting impact. Through live events, classroom programs, community outreach programs, and public art, the foundation builds layers of knowledge, understanding, and empathy to inspire the public to act as better stewards of their coasts and water resources. Just as important, we hope to instill an understanding of human impacts on our water with a particular emphasis on non-point pollution problems and solutions.

These goals could not be achieved without the tireless efforts of world-class science institutions, such as our educational partners, the Scripps Institution of Oceanography (UCSD) and the Birch Aquarium at Scripps, where scientists are currently codeveloping the Wyland Ocean Challenge, "Clean Water for the 21st Century . . . and Beyond," a free nationwide classroom education program. By bringing together groups from far-reaching disciplines in art, science, and conservation, we have an opportunity to fundamentally change perceptions of a healthy environment. We can demonstrate the value—and the beauty—of our planet, and encourage preservation for future generations. Joining us in these efforts are the American Zoo and Aquarium Association, Project AWARE, and the Surfrider Foundation, as well as hundreds of community service organizations, companies, and concerned citizens.

On a personal note, the authors would like to thank all those who made this book possible, starting with the courageous and dedicated people who brought environmental issues to the public consciousness. People like Rachel Carson and Dr. Sylvia Earle, for whom this book is dedicated, and others like Bob Hunter, a cofounder of Greenpeace.

But sustaining our blue planet is not the sole province of the "environmentalists." Others, like explorer Robert Ballard, who show us the amazing inner worlds of our oceans, lakes, streams, and rivers, do as much to capture our attention and reveal the inherent magnificence of these places and the wonders within them. Finally, there is the matter of water for our very survival and the plight of water in the third world—a condition that is now seeing a glimmer of hope thanks to the work of the United Nations Environment Programme, the World Health Organization, and countless nongovernmental organizations.

On the practical side of things, the authors thank everyone who oversaw the direct creation of this book, from Holly Kent, executive director of the Alaska Waterways Council, to Gregg Hamby, Jennifer Martin, Deana Duffek, the entire Wyland design team, and Dorothy O'Brien and the rest of our friends at Andrews McMeel. Of course, none of this would be possible without the vision of Angela Needham and the staff of Wyland Worldwide.

Introduction

Congratulations. You made it this far. You saw the cover of this book, and thought, "Maybe it's time I learned what this conservation stuff is all about." Maybe you saw the book in the store, passed by it a few times, waited until no one was looking, then thumbed through a few pages. So far so good, right? And really, what's the harm? After all, we're talking about the environment here. We're talking about your kids, your spouse, your grandchildren, your neighbors, your pet iguana, your ficus. All of which exist in large part because of our planet's marvelous system of water. Fortunately, we're blessed with lots of this stuff. It's in our oceans, lakes, streams, rivers, ponds, wetlands, aquifers, clouds, the air around us, and even our own bodies. Some parts of the world have more of it than others, but take it all away, and this great global oasis changes dramatically. Who knows? Perhaps in a million years, some extraterrestrial intelligence may zoom by our planet, sending out probes and cute little motorcar-shaped robots, and only after months and months of study, determine that the big barren rift dividing the eastern and the western parts of the North American continent was once a vast flowing river. Or that the big clump of divots to the north were some very big lakes, perhaps even "great!" lakes, if the ETs are prone to Madison Avenue hype.

But why let things get that far? There's plenty each of us can do to keep our planet blue. All you need is a little information and an occasional reminder. In the next few pages, we're going to explain a few things about water: why it's here, what it does, where it goes after it collects all the goo from your toothpaste, and how it usually—but not always—comes back clean. Best of all, we'll show you a few easy things that you and your family can do to help it along.

People think water is free because it falls from the sky. Well, it is—but treated, filtered, and piped water isn't.

—ANDREW SEIDEL, president, USFilter

Unfortunately, because of the brief length of this book, we've had to omit certain chemical formulas, a great deal of physics, and a few ponderous philosophies from people you have never heard of—but we will gladly reinstate this information, upon request. We'll even provide a few facts that you can throw out at dinner parties, like the fact that two-thirds of the world is covered by water, and only a small amount of that is drinkable. Or that somewhere in the world, at this very moment, a kid named Ralph is filling balloons with water and will seek retribution on his sister for taking his bike to the mall without his permission. (This may or may not result in other social issues, which will not be covered in this book.)

Okay, you're probably thinking: *I know, I know, water is important. We have to keep it clean. It's where fish live. Hockey players skate on it. And it looks nice cascading in a white mist down Niagara Falls. But how does that really affect me or my swimming pool or, for that matter, my new modern art sculpture that flings streams of water in the shape of my family crest?* The answer is simple: It depends. Our planet is certainly blessed with an abundance of water. So much so that we are still uncovering information about it. We discover new species of aquatic critters every day. But perhaps most important, we have reached a point of globalization in which everything we do affects someone or something else. Call it the age of interconnectedness. And nothing symbolizes our dependence upon one another more than the interconnected state of our planet's water.

Storing and selling water will be the key to California's future.

—MARK LIGGET, senior vice president, Cadiz Inc.

What is a need for water?

At its most basic level, we each need about five liters of water a day to survive. In our communities, we ask only that the water is clean, free from contamination, and that we have access to it. This seems to be a reasonable request, and it is most often met in the United States and other industrialized nations. But for billions of people around the world that is far from the case. Access to clean, safe water is precarious at best. Poor regions around the world lack the money, technology, natural resources, and political will to ensure adequate supplies of water. In 2000, nearly one billion people in rural areas around the world did not have access to basic water services. A staggering 2.6 billion people in those areas did not have access to most of the sanitation services we take for granted, running the risk of a wicked cocktail of waterborne diseases, including typhoid, cholera, dysentery, malaria, and viral hepatitis A. In 1998, thirty-one countries faced chronic freshwater shortages. In twenty years, forty-eight countries are expected to face shortages, affecting more than 2.8 billion people.

But those are someone else's problems, right? Not exactly. In our own country, arsenic from industry and mining in poor communities has created another set of health problems. And, as we mentioned, the world has entered a new stage in which one country's problems now become everyone's problems. The World Health Organization has undertaken an enormous yet simple mission of promoting three key hygiene behaviors: hand washing with soap, safe disposal of human waste, and safe water handling and storage. With growing populations and increasing demands for water, simple steps like these actually increase the availability of safe water for everyone.

That, in a proverbial nutshell, is the heart of this book. We need water, but the future of our supply is not guaranteed, so how our generation—and the generations after us—thrive will depend on how we maintain our water resources, how we use them, allocate them, and treat them.

The idea of water as an economic and social good, and who controls this water and whether it is clean enough to drink, are going to be major issues in the country.

—Economist GARY WOLFF

The other part of this book recognizes an entirely separate fact: We are sharing this planet with countless plants and animals. These living things are as dependent on water as we are, perhaps even more so. Plants have a wonderful ability to turn carbon dioxide and water into food. In turn, they give us oxygen. This exchange of carbon dioxide between animals and plants keeps our entire biosphere intact. Without water, this miraculous process is destroyed. And, unfortunately, so goes humanity. We've seen climate change around the world in the last fifty years, as water is relocated, overallocated, and polluted. Entire ecosystems have changed—and the way of life in entire regions has changed. But does it have to continue this way? Plants and animals in the Mojave, Sonoran, and Great Basin deserts are exquisitely adapted to store water and minimize evaporation loss in extremely harsh conditions in regions that are deceptively rich with life.

You think we have bad fights over oil? Just wait until we start fighting over water. It's predicted in the Koran.

—Anonymous Jordanian quoted in the *Washington Post,* March 28, 1991

The lessons are there. Nature adapts. And there is no reason why we shouldn't follow its lead—after all, it did pretty well before we arrived. (With our apologies to the dinosaurs, of course.) Now, it is up to us. In the United States, the Bureau of Land Management, the National Park Service, the Fish and Wildlife Service, and private groups and individuals are taking steps to consider the health of entire ecosystems. Groups like the World Health Organization and UNESCO have embraced environmental concerns in their efforts to improve the lives of others. To these groups, water is everything. It is the basic need that must be met before all others. It is the ultimate source of life. In the southwestern United States, where a running spring once meant the difference between survival or death to a settler, an adage went, "Whiskey's fer drinkin'. Water's fer fightin' over." Now, as this resource becomes more precious, as we dam and divert rivers, as we pump aquifers and try to tame dry deserts, we are faced with a challenge: to hold the water of our planet with the reverence and respect it deserves. For this simple element, so necessary, yet so often misunderstood, holds the key to our lives and the health of our planet.

Always drink upstream from the herd.

—Cowboy proverb

Part I

Getting Your Feet Wet

1

It's So Big

For sheer size, it's hard to beat the incredible volume of water that exists on our planet. If you filled a glass with all the water in the world, the glass would have to be seven hundred miles high and seven hundred miles wide. (And if you think that's hard to swallow, just remember that's all the water we've ever had—or will ever have.)

The trouble with water—and there is trouble with water—is that they're not making any more of it. They're not making any less, mind you, but no more either. There is the same amount of water on the planet now as there was in prehistoric times. People, however, they're making more of—many more, far more than is ecologically sensible—and all those people are utterly dependent on water for their lives (humans consist mostly of water), for their livelihoods, their food, and increasingly, their industry. Humans can live for a month without food but will die in less than a week without water. Humans consume water, discard it, poison it, waste it, and restlessly change the hydrological cycles, indifferent to the consequences: too many people, too little water, water in the wrong places and in the wrong amounts.

—MARQ DE VILLIERS,
Water: The Fate of Our Most Precious Resource, 2000

FACT

97.5 percent of all the water on earth is undrinkable seawater. Of the remaining 2.5 percent, nearly two-thirds is locked up in polar ice caps. The remaining third is all ours, except half of that is considered polluted by most international standards.

2

It's So Wet

Okay, so maybe you want to know a little chemistry. Water consists of two parts hydrogen and one part oxygen. There's no shortage of these elements in the universe. Yet, for reasons that remain largely unknown, very few planets have such an abundance of liquid water. One theory suggests that the earth was basically pelted early on by extraterrestrial snowballs the size of Manhattan. As things heated up, the ice melted, and oceans formed.

Water is fundamental for life and health. The human right to water is indispensable for leading a healthy life in human dignity. It is a prerequisite to the realization of all other human rights.

—THE UNITED NATIONS COMMITTEE ON ECONOMIC, CULTURAL AND SOCIAL RIGHTS, Environment News Service, November 27, 2002

Water is the basis of life and the blue arteries of the earth! Everything in the nonmarine environment depends on freshwater to survive.

—SANDRA POSTEL, "Global Water Policy Project," *Grist Magazine,* April 26, 2004

FACT

Water is the essential ingredient to life as we know it—and most likely a common requirement for life elsewhere. Scientists believe that Europa, an ice-encrusted moon of Jupiter, may contain life because it has heat from volcanic activity to maintain liquid water and dissolve chemicals essential for living organisms.

3

Now That I'm on the Water Cycle, How Do I Get Off?

Our advice is: Once you find a good thing, stick with it. Our water cycle has given us a pretty good ride for millions of years. It's like a self-cleaning sprinkler system with four parts. Each part involves changing the state of the water. And as it passes from state to state, it generally becomes purer. For example, as it evaporates, it becomes a gas. When things cool down, it liquefies again and, with some help from gravity, falls back to earth as rain, where it collects into lakes, rivers, and aquifers.

O nly 2.5 percent of the world's water is not salty, and two-thirds of that is trapped in the icecaps and glaciers. Of what is left, about 20 percent is in remote areas, and most of the rest comes at the wrong time and in the wrong place, as with monsoons and floods. The amount of freshwater available for human use is less than 0.08 percent of all the water on the planet. About 70 percent of the freshwater is already used for agriculture, and a recent World Water Council report says the demands of industry and energy will grow rapidly. The report estimates that in the next two decades the use of water by humans will increase by about 40 percent, and that 17 percent more water than is available will be needed to grow the world's food. . . . The commission concludes that "only rapid and imaginative institutional and technological innovation can avoid the crisis."

—"Water Arithmetic 'Doesn't Add Up,'"
BBC News, March 13, 2000

Even the Trees
Are in on It

We've long known that plants have been muscling in on our water. But it turns out, they're giving as good as they're getting. Besides giving off oxygen (which we think is really terrific of them!), many plants go the extra mile by removing harmful chemicals, like nitrogen and phosphorus, before they reach our rivers, lakes, and aquifers.

Every human should have the idea of taking care of the environment, of nature, of water. So using too much or wasting water should have some kind of feeling or sense of concern. Some sort of responsibility and with that, a sense of discipline.

—The fourteenth Dalai Lama, TENZIN GYATSO

Some plants such as flax, lupin, and hebe grow on tailings from abandoned mines, extracting significant levels of arsenic and lead. Others such as alpine pennycress accumulate organic chemicals, heavy metals, and other toxins from water. Using plants to do this kind of dirty work is called phytoremediation.

While you can't randomly expect any plant to clean up a toxic waste site, many home and garden centers provide a range of plants that can beautify your home—and do their part for your local water system.

5

What Is a Dead Zone, Anyway?

This should not be confused with a famous district in San Francisco where a bunch of tie-dyed musicians launched a new era in hippie music. Dead zones are oxygen-depleted coastal areas created by nutrient-rich runoff. While you might think an abundance of nutrients benefits marine life, it actually feeds huge blooms of algae that are digested by microorganisms when they die. This process sucks up vast amounts of oxygen—leaving little for the remaining plants and animals.

I understood when I was just a child that without water, everything dies. I didn't understand until much later that no one "owns" water. It might rise on your property, but it just passes through. You can use it, and abuse it, but it is not yours to own. It is part of the global commons, not "property" but part of our life support system.

—MARQ DE VILLIERS, *Water: The Fate of Our Most Precious Resource*, 2000

A river seems a magic thing. A magic, moving, living part of the very earth itself.

—LAURA GILPIN, *The Rio Grande: River of Destiny*, 1949

6

Only Chumps Dump

Nothing makes your car purr like fresh motor oil. Mechanics recommend an oil change every six months, and that used oil has to go somewhere. Unfortunately, that's often down a storm drain. Dumping out one quart of used motor oil can pollute 250,000 gallons of water.

We have a lot of ways to meet our energy needs. These salmon only have one river forever. If we do not support them, they will go extinct.

—TODD TRUE, attorney with the Earthjustice Legal Defense Fund in Washington, D.C, as quoted in *Seattle Post-Intelligencer,* May 4, 2001

A nation that fails to plan intelligently for the development and protection of its precious waters will be condemned to wither because of its shortsightedness. The hard lessons of history are clear, written on the deserted sands and ruins of once proud civilizations.

—LYNDON B. JOHNSON (1908-1973) thirty-sixth president of the United States, "Letter to the President of the Senate and to the Speaker of the House Transmitting an Assessment of the Nation's Water Resources," November 18, 1968

FACT

A few years ago, the infamous Exxon *Valdez* oil spill created one of the worst environmental disasters in history. But did you know that every eight months the same of amount of oil (10.9 million gallons) spills from leaky cars and improperly discarded motor oil into storm drains? From there, it's into our streams and rivers, and eventually, out to sea.

Almost all oil-change shops will recycle your used oil. The U.S. Environmental Protection Agency says that if all Americans recycled their oil—the equivalent of 120 supertankers—it would supply enough motor oil for fifty million cars a year.

7

Shower Power

It's too bad that most Americans don't have to fetch water by the bucket because those of us who enjoy long, luxuriating showers would be in the best shape of our lives, especially since the average five-minute shower uses twenty-five to fifty gallons of water.

With respect to water, Canadians and Americans suffer from the same disease: We say that it is priceless, but act as if it were absurdly cheap. Most North Americans pay far less for their water than even just the cost of supplying it, cleaning it up, and returning it to the environment. Yet subsidizing water use is economically and ecologically disastrous. In fact, heavy subsidization of water in the U.S. is the cause of any water "shortages" that may exist there.

—"Will Foreigners Drink Canada Dry?," *Toronto Globe and Mail,* May 23, 1998

Install a low-flow showerhead. You won't be giving up as much as you think. Aerated low-flow shower-heads reduce the water needed for a shower, but maintain the pressure you like by mixing it with air. So you can still indulge without the guilt.

8

The Car Wash Blues

Driveways are good places for parking cars, not cleaning them. All those soapy suds find their way into storm drains, and, as you might have guessed by now, they don't end up back in the bottle.

According to the 2000 U.S. Census, 138 million registered automobiles drive the roads of America today. Nearly half of those vehicles are washed each month—requiring up to 4.4 billion gallons of water.

TIP

Take your car to a commercial car wash. These facilities must meet stringent requirements from the Environmental Protection Agency for disposal of wastewater. They also use about thirty-two gallons per wash, whereas washing your car at home can use up to twice that amount. Or wash your car on your lawn—you won't have to water that day and the grass and dirt act like a filter to keep the suds out of local water bodies.

9

The Inside Poop on Pet Waste

What a great dog you have! You walk him, play with him, and feed him the very best food. In return, you get unconditional love and mint-condition love droppings, if you know what we mean. Unfortunately, pet waste runs off into the storm drains directly into local water bodies, making it dangerous for swimming or drinking. It can also contaminate shellfish beds.

Anyone Can Spell C-A-T

But can you pronounce these diseases that are passed from pet waste to humans?

Campylobacteriosis. A bacterial infection carried by dogs and cats that frequently causes diarrhea in humans.

Salmonellosis. The most common bacterial infection transmitted to humans by other animals. Symptoms include fever, muscle aches, headache, vomiting, and diarrhea.

Toxocariasis. Roundworms usually transmitted from dogs to humans, often without noticeable symptoms, but may cause vision loss, a rash, fever, or cough.

Toxoplasmosis. A parasite carried by cats that can cause birth defects if a woman becomes infected during pregnancy. Can also be a problem for people with depressed immune systems.

TIP

Dispose of pet waste properly—or, as we like to say, scoop the poop.

10

How Does Your Garden Grow?

If it's with chemical fertilizers and pesticides, you might want to consider other alternatives. Runoff from these garden treatments is among the leading contaminants of our water systems.

Industrial agriculture now accounts for over half of America's water pollution. Two years ago, Pfiesteria outbreaks connected with wastes from industrial chicken factories forced the closure of two major tributaries of the Chesapeake and threatened Maryland's vital shellfish industry. Tyson Foods has polluted half of all streams in northwestern Arkansas with so much fecal bacteria that swimming is prohibited. Drugs and hormones needed to keep confined animals alive and growing are mainly excreted with the wastes and saturate local waterways.

—ROBERT F. KENNEDY JR., "Free-Range at Last, Free-Range at Last," *Grist Magazine,* November 20, 2000

According to the EPA, at least seventy-four pesticides have been found in the groundwater of thirty-eight states. And we're not the only ones who feel the effects. The National Marine Fisheries Service, the agency charged with carrying out Endangered Species Act regulations for listed salmon, has indicated serious concern about the effects of pesticides on salmon in the Pacific Northwest. Trace amounts of at least one commonly used insecticide—diazinon—can affect a salmon's nervous system in levels as low as one to ten parts per billion.

Of the billion pounds of pesticides used each year in the United States, less than 1 percent reaches a pest.

Try organics. Many home and garden stores have great alternatives to chemical pesticides, such as ladybugs to control aphids, and compost fertilizers that build healthy gardens and help reduce solid waste in landfills.

11

Wanted: More Graffiti

We're not talking about your signature in giant purple block letters. But a storm drain stenciling campaign that lets everyone know these drainage systems are designed to prevent floods—not provide a receptacle for used motor oil, cigarette butts, straws, and little Jimmy's plastic boat.

Filthy water cannot be washed.

—West African proverb

Our stewardship of the earth is brief. We owe it to those who follow to keep that in perspective, to be responsible passengers along the way.

—GEORGE H.W. BUSH, forty-first president of the United States

In a heavy rain, a well-maintained storm drain system can divert millions of cubic feet of water away from neighborhoods and into local reservoirs, lakes, rivers, and out to sea.

Explain to your children or neighbors the benefits of storm drains—and that chemicals and debris poured into them go straight to our streams, lakes, and oceans. And while you're at it, you might remind them that they're also not a one-way ticket to freedom for Millie, the family goldfish.

BONUS TIP: Try some storm-drain stenciling yourself. Join the Center for Marine Conservation's "Storm Drain Sentries" program. Get your stencil for free at the CMC Web site at http://www.oceanconservancy.org.

12

Jellies on a Roll

Imagine going to your favorite seafood restaurant, ordering the special of the day—and getting a plateful of jellyfish. As fisheries become more depleted, scientists warn that one of the consequences may be an explosion in jellyfish populations. Hardy survivors, jellyfish thrive on food sources created by excessive nitrate runoff from farms, and they are now experiencing a surge from the absence of natural predators.

TIP

Jellyfish may seem a long way from America's breadbasket, but such strange links exist, especially in marine areas affected by agricultural runoff. What's more, before contaminants like nitrates and phosphates even hit the ocean, they can affect our rivers, streams, and groundwater, and cause serious illness. But why settle for that? As farming practices around the world improve, so will the quality of our soil, air, water—and, ultimately, the quality of life. You can play a part in this turnaround by asking policymakers to demand reductions in harmful farm chemicals and support smarter, healthier, sustainable agriculture, such as crop rotations, soil-enriching cover crops, and alternative pesticides. Even if you're a city slicker who couldn't grow a weed if you tried, a little more awareness about how food gets to your table can sow the seeds of health for future generations.

FACT

Usually found in the Pacific Ocean, the Australian spotted jellyfish has broadened its range to include fish breeding areas in the Gulf of Mexico. The intruders are eating huge numbers of larvae of Spanish mackerel, menhaden, and other fish that are vital to the economy of the region.

Heavy fertilizer use near the Black Sea fueled a huge dead zone in the 1970s—causing a decline in many fish species and, like in the Gulf of Mexico, paved the way for an invasion of comb jellies. In an odd twist, with the fall of communism—and the region's economy—agricultural spending on fertilizer declined and nitrate runoff into the Black Sea plummeted. Now, experts say, the Black Sea's ecology has shown signs of recovery.

My soul is full of longing
For the secret of the Sea,
And the heart of the great ocean
Sends a thrilling pulse through me.

—HENRY WADSWORTH
LONGFELLOW
(1807-1882), "The Secret of the Sea"

13

Bottle Bashing

Fish wouldn't last long without water. And neither would you or I. The trouble is in our race to stay hydrated Americans discard 2.5 million plastic water bottles every hour.

The frog does not
Drink up
The pond in which
He lives.

—American Indian proverb quoted in
Water Wasteland by DAVID ZWICK and MARCY
BENSTOCK, 1971

TIP

Spring for a reusable water bottle and fill it with tap water before you leave the house. One quarter of those fancy bottled water brands are filtered water from the tap anyway. If taste is still a factor, add a reverse osmosis filter. A filter lowers the flow, resulting in less water waste.

14

If You Love It, Set It Free

There are few wonders of engineering more marvelous than a dam. These structures span some of our greatest rivers, generating electricity, providing irrigation and flood control, and creating huge reservoirs. Many are essential to our communities. Others, however, could be replaced with more environmentally friendly structures and new technologies or eliminated entirely—with no harm to the community.

When we talk of flood control, we usually think of dams and deeper river channels to impound the waters or hurry their runoff. Yet neither is the ultimate solution, simply because floods are caused by the flow of water downhill. If the hills are wooded, that flow is checked. If there is a swamp at the foot of the hills, the swamp sponges up most of the excess water, restores some of it to the underground water supply, and feeds the remainder slowly into the streams. Strip the hills, drain the boglands, and you create flood conditions inevitably. Yet that is what we have been doing for years.

—HAL BORLAND,
Sundial of the Seasons, 1964l

If none have been conducted within the last five years, insist on an updated economic and environmental impact study on any dams in your area.

15

The Great Weight Debate

Americans produce an average of four pounds of trash per person, per day. If you have a calculator on hand, you know what that means. And, yes, we know old habits can be tough to break. But it's easier to lighten up than you might think!

Humans build their societies around consumption of fossil water long buried in the earth, and these societies, being based on temporary resources, face the problem of being temporary themselves.

—CHARLES BOWDEN, *Killing the Hidden Waters*, 1977

It is estimated that in the United States a population of ten thousand people generates enough waste in a year to fill an acre ten feet deep. That means in a large American city of three million people, approximately three hundred acres of land are buried ten feet deep each year.

Donate reusable goods, recycle what you can, and stop buying things that have so much packaging. If each household canceled ten mail-order catalogs it would reduce trash by 3.5 pounds per year. (If everybody did this, the stack of canceled catalogs would be two thousand miles high.)

BONUS TIP: Give your mailbox a breather by cutting back on its junk-mail intake. Contact the Direct Marketing Association and tell them to take you off their mailing lists. They'll stop your name from being sold to most large mailing list companies—and you'll reduce your junk mail by up to 75 percent. Write to: Mail Preference Service, Direct Marketing Association, PO Box 643, Carmel NY 10512. Or visit them at http://www.dmaconsumers.org/off-mailinglist.html.

16

Start a "Pee Outside" Day or "If It's Yellow, Let It Mellow"

Our reporters in the field have learned that Stigomta, Sweden, has an annual "Pee Outside" Day, where nobody flushes a toilet all day. This event cuts the water usage of the town in half for the day.

A Note from the Land of Sky-Blue Waters

Beer. The perfect accessory to an afternoon on the couch. But did you know that many pesticides and chemicals are used to grow the barley, hops, apples and other ingredients that went into making over 223 million barrels of beer in 2004? Now, unless you've got a chronic fruit fly problem, you probably want to limit your pesticide intake. So, may we suggest an organic beer: It's got the flavor you like, without all the "bonus" chemicals.

FACT

One day a year, beer sales in Stigomta, Sweden, mysteriously decline.

TIP

The average toilet flush uses three to seven gallons of water. We're not saying never flush. (In certain circumstances a double flush may even be required.) But, well, you decide.

BONUS TIP: Place a sealed plastic bottle in your toilet tank. Keep it safely away from any operating mechanisms and save up to 15 percent of the water you use with each flush.

17
A Cure for Buildup

Everyone knows you have to break a few eggs to make an omelet. But all the dirt, drywall, paint, and other stuff that goes into home improvements can degrade local rivers, lakes, and even the ocean, if you hose it down the storm drain.

The U.S. water supply is laced with residues of hundreds of medicinal and household chemicals, compounds that originate not at a Dow Chemical drainage pipe but from our own personal plumbing. The contaminants come from our bladders and bowels, our bathtub drains and kitchen sinks. As much as 90 percent of anything the doctor orders you to swallow passes out of your body and into your toilet. Wastes from farm animals are never treated—and loaded with antibiotics and fertility hormones. As chemists make new concoctions, the water supply takes the hit.

—MARK D. UEHLING, "Free Drugs from Your Faucet," *Salon,* October 25, 2001

FACT

Many people end up with an abundance of hazardous waste materials in their house simply from buying more than they need. Planning projects carefully, using alternatives to hazardous materials, and donating leftover materials are great ways to minimize the impact from home improvements.

TIP

Put sandbags, absorbent material, or hay bales around your work site at home to avoid washing toxic materials into the storm drains. And remind those high-priced contractors to haul the gunk away and dispose of it properly.

BONUS TIP: Put some color in someone else's life. Donate your leftover paint to a local church, community group, or theater group, or others in need. If you still have leftover solvent-based paint, don't throw it out with normal trash—save it for your local hazardous waste collection program.

18

Beat the Wrap

Is it a package or an onion? With so many layers of plastic around products these days, it's often hard to tell.

The Environmental Protection Agency on Thursday released a report confirming the bad news: that America's so-called Great Waters—the Great Lakes, Chesapeake Bay, Lake Champlain, and coastal waters—continue to suffer from runoff, pollution discharge, and air pollution. According to the Great Waters Report, fish consumption advisories have been in place for thirty-nine of the fifty-six Great Waters since 1997. "Although the United States has made tremendous progress cleaning up its water by removing billions of pounds of pollutants and doubling the number of waterways safe for fishing and swimming, a majority of Americans live within ten miles of a polluted lake, river, stream, or coastal area," said EPA Administrator Carol Browner.

—"U.S. Economy Depends on Clean Water," Environmental News Network, June 9, 2000

FACT

Americans use enough plastic wrap each year to shrink-wrap the state of Texas. Unfortunately, the production of some plastic exposes substantial amounts of toxic chemicals such as *ethylene oxide, benzene,* and *xylenes* to air and water.

According to the Earthworks Group, if 10 percent of Americans purchased products with less plastic wrapping 10 percent of the time, we could eliminate 144 million pounds of plastic from our landfills, reduce industrial pollution, and send a message to manufacturers that we're serious about alternatives.

TIP

Recycle plastic package wrapping or, better still, choose products with less wrapping or recyclable packaging. You'll reduce solid waste in your area—what we call "source reduction"—and everyone benefits from that.

Part II

What Are You Calling a Bad Habit?

19

Hold on to Your Butt

Smoke 'em if you got 'em. That's up to you. Just dispose of cigarette butts where they belong.

In California each year, tobacco smoke releases into the environment 40 tons of nicotine, 365 tons of particulate matter, and 1,900 tons of carbon monoxide, not to mention benzene and arsenic–and that's in a state where smoking is on the decline.

FACT

Cigarettes are the most littered item in the world. More than 130 million butts were tossed out last year in Texas alone. As they degrade, these harmless-looking pellets release toxic compounds that infiltrate our drinking water and poison wildlife.

TIP

Know someone who sets Olympic distance records for flicking cigarettes out their car window? Gently remind them that they've just sent their butt on the slow train to the storm drain—and guess where that dumps off?

20

Beware of Things That Go Drip in the Night

Besides keeping you awake, a faucet that drips a drop a second is leaking 2,600 gallons of water a year. Here's what we say: Get some good sleep, save some money . . . fix the drip.

20 percent of all the toilets in American homes are leaking right now.

A leaky faucet is one of the easiest, most inexpensive household repairs you can make.

Low-flow faucet aerators, toilet dams, and minor repairs in your bathroom can save a family of four between ten thousand to twenty-five thousand gallons of water every year.

21

Fish Don't Get Depressed, So Why Are We Giving Them Prozac?

Share your love for clean water by not sharing your prescription drugs. Designed to dissolve quickly for rapid absorption by our bodies, these drugs can't be filtered by most sewage treatment plants.

[A] survey of more than one hundred waterways downstream from treatment plants and animal feedlots in thirty states found minute amounts of dozens of antibiotics, hormones, pain relievers, cough suppressants, disinfectants, and other products. It is not known whether they are harmful to plants, animals, or people. The findings were released yesterday on the Web site of the United States Geological Survey, which conducted the research, and in an online journal, *Environmental Science and Technology*. Additional federal studies are under way to see if any contamination reaches taps or groundwater used for drinking, but the program under which they are conducted, the toxic substances hydrology program of the geological survey, is slated to be eliminated under budget cuts proposed by the Bush administration, government officials said. "As we look more at low levels of drugs, it appears that some of them have real biological effects in real situations," said Dr. Rebecca Goldburg, a senior scientist at Environmental Defense, a private lobbying and research group. About 40 percent of the streams in the study showed traces of estrogen or other reproductive hormones.

—ANDREW C. REVKIN, "FDA Considers New Tests for Environmental Effects," *New York Times,* March 14, 2002

FACT

Fish and other aquatic wildlife are starting to show up with high levels of human drugs in their bodies. If this continues your doctor might advise you to eat a salmon a day instead of writing a prescription.

Dispose of your prescriptions properly; don't flush them.

22

Seconds Anyone?

Imagine the world's water being served on a giant dinner table. Imagine everyone in the world enjoying a cool, refreshing glass. Now imagine a few million unexpected guests show up. Then a few million more. . . .

In the late 1990s a handful of conglomerates began to quietly acquire control of the world's water systems. As the value of water began to soar, multi-billion-dollar firms such as Vivendi, Suez, Enron, and Bechtel scoured the world in pursuit of lucrative business opportunities. Between 1994 and 1998 there were 139 water-related deals worth an aggregate of nearly $4 billion. In a period of six months in 1999 Vivendi bought the western American water operator USFilter for $6.2 billion, and Suez purchased the East Coast company United Water Resources for $1 billion. Those two transactions came right after Enron paid $2.2 billion for the British utility Wessex Water. At the same time, electronic water auctions were launched on the Internet. At sites like water2water.com and water-rights.com, individuals with excess water (such as farmers with irrigation contracts) could put their water rights up for sale to the highest private bidder. As a result of all of these different deals and ventures, hundreds of millions of people worldwide now depend on transnationals (companies based thousands of miles away) for their water supplies.

—Edited from JEFFREY ROTHFEDER's
Every Drop for Sale, 2001, quoted in the *Ecologist,*
March 2004

FACT

The USDA says that the average American ate nearly two hundred pounds of red meat in 2000—a hefty fifty-seven pounds more than average meat consumption in the 1950s. It takes up to 2,500 gallons of water to grow and process a pound of beef. This means that in this country, in a single year, an average of half a million gallons of water is invested in the steaks, burgers, and ribs eaten by just one person.

Demand for water has tripled over the last half century. With that in mind, remember: Water is a finite resource—and every drop we use is a drop from someone else's cup.

TIP

Consider its use wisely.

23

Water Color: The Politics of Conservation

In 1970, the White House and Congress actually agreed on something and created the Environmental Protection Agency (EPA). These days, if you think blue, then you probably think this agency isn't doing quite enough and tends to underestimate the role water plays in the functioning of our planet's ecosystems. If you think red, then you probably think this agency does too much and is extremely accurate in its assessments.

But we have not used our waters well. Our major rivers are defiled by noxious debris. Pollutants from cities and industries kill the fish in our streams. Many waterways are covered with oil slicks and contain growths of algae that destroy productive life and make the water unfit for recreation. "Polluted Water—No Swimming" has become a familiar sign on too many beaches and rivers. A lake that has served many generations of men now can be destroyed by man in less than one generation.

—LYNDON B. JOHNSON (1908-1973),
thirty-sixth president of the United States, Special
Message to Congress, "To Renew a Nation,"
March 8, 1968

Clean water is not an expenditure of federal funds; clean water is an investment in the future of our country.

—BUD SHUSTER, U.S. Representative,
quoted in the *Washington Post,* January 9, 1987

FACT

From whatever side you look at it, the EPA has estimated that one-third of all the waters tested in the United States are unsafe for fishing, swimming, and drinking. Red or blue, if you join a group or give money to a group that is working to protect water quality, you are protecting water quality—no red or blue about it.

TIP

If you're not sure what we mean by thinking blue and red, then you probably don't even know there is an EPA and you can skip to the next chapter.

24

Try Green Cleaning

You've probably figured out by now that if everybody reading this book made one small environmental change in their life—the net effect to the planet would be huge. A new wave of "green cleaners" do the same job as synthetic cleaning products without all the harm to the environment. Synthetic cleaning additives like petrochemical optical brighteners are difficult to break down, both in water purification systems and in rivers and lakes. They may cause allergic reactions in people, they can cause mutations in bacteria that inhibit biodegradability, and they are toxic to aquatic life. Others, like synthetic fabric softeners, introduce phosphates into the water systems that lead to algae blooms that lead to oxygen depletion and—you probably saw this coming–lead to a bunch of dead fish.

FACT: About half of all cleaning services on the West Coast feature cleaning with nontoxic products as a main business or as a premium service.

Our nation could save eighty-two thousand barrels of oil a year if every household in the United States replaced just one bottle of twenty-eight-ounce petroleum-based dishwashing liquid with a nontoxic vegetable-based product. That's enough oil to drive a car over eighty-six million miles.

Switch to vegetable-based cleaning products. (No, this doesn't mean swabbing your linoleum with a head of cabbage.) Parsley, orange oil, corn, and sugar-beet derivatives are a few of the natural substances that are being substituted for synthetics. As demand grows, even some of the big chains, like Giant, Safeway, Whole Foods, and Trader Joe's, are now stocking shelves with natural cleaning alternatives.

A Fish Tale

Once upon a time there was a type of fish that was really yummy and people loved to eat it. Fishermen caught more of the fish and then more people found out about it and wanted to eat it, so fishermen caught even more of that fish and even more people found out about it and it became downright "trendy" to eat it.

Soon, people began paying a lot of money for that special fish and fishermen caught more and more and more of them until one day, the fishermen were having a hard time finding any of the special fish. The scientists were called to do a study and discovered that there weren't very many of the fish left. The scientists talked to the government on behalf of the remaining fish. The government felt bad and said, "It is illegal to catch this type of fish."

The fish rejoiced and were relieved because they thought they would have a chance to rebuild their families, but something strange was happening—the fish kept disappearing! So a couple of brave fish went to the towns to see what was happening and lo and behold, restaurants were still serving the special fish—they were still on the menu!

The fish were extremely puzzled and since these were very brave fish, they decided to talk to a wise fisherman. They asked the fisherman, "How can restaurants still be serving us up when the government said it was illegal to catch us?" The wise fisherman told the fish, "You misunderstand. Legal fishermen can't catch you now, but illegal fishermen can." The fish were still puzzled and asked, "Shouldn't it be illegal to serve us if it is illegal to catch us?" The wise fisherman gave a wise, sad smile and said, "Shouldn't it be indeed. . . ."

Colonel Halibut in the Library with a Fishing Pole

In the children's game Clue, players try to solve a mystery by looking for weapons, motives, and, of course, a culprit. In 2000, Congress took the same approach to the mystery of declining fisheries around U.S. waters. They commissioned scientists, elected officials, and fisherman to study the quality of ocean life within a 4½ million-square-mile area. After three years, the Pew Commission concluded that overfishing was leading to a dwindling supply of once-common fish.

FACT: Most of the problems associated with overfishing have occurred in the last fifty years by rapid advances in fishing technology. Huge factory ships emerged in the '50s and '60s that could stay at sea for weeks, with equipment to freeze or tin fish, and return home only when their holds were full. The results to fisheries are hardly suprising. But with reduced customer demand and international agreements limiting catches, we can still ensure the future of this valuable resource.

Severely depleted along the Atlantic, striped bass have made a striking comeback when given a chance to recover. North Atlantic swordfish did the same in response to lower catch limits and closed nursery areas. Fish communities returned to marine habitats around the nation after waste discharges were reduced.

The Pew Commission has numerous recommendations to improve the health of marine fisheries, but there are plenty of easy things you can do, as well. Take a moment to visit http://www.seafoodwatch.org to learn which fish are endangered, and don't order them when you eat out—you'll help the fish and the fishermen that are doing the right thing. (You'll learn more about this in number 39.)

I'm Melting in the Rain

It may have a catchy name, but acid rain is nothing to sing about. It forms when emissions from fossil fuel-burning sources (like your car or some factory smoke stacks) meet water vapor. If you live in the northern East Coast of the United States you are probably all too familiar with the signs of acid rain—limestone brick buildings that look like they are melting, scarred trees, and lakes that are so acidic that swimming in them would be like taking a bath in vinegar (and of course, nothing can live in that).

Let the rain kiss you.
Let the rain beat upon your head with
silver liquid drops.
Let the rain sing you a lullaby.

The rain makes still pools on the
sidewalk.
The rain makes running pools in the
gutter.
The rain plays a little sleep-song on our
roof at night—

And I love the rain.

—LANGSTON HUGHES (1902-1967),
"April Rain Song," 1921

FACT

Congress passed the Clean Air Act of 1972 to try to cut back on the amount of air pollution that causes acid rain. In only a few decades, this has resulted in a significant reduction in the release of airborne sulfur dioxide and nitrogen oxides—two gases that form acid rain.

TIP

So what can you do? Make sure your car is properly maintained and not spewing clouds of black smoke—or better yet, why not buy a hybrid?

How the
Other Half Lives

America is among the most water-rich nations in the world. The average American household uses 100 to 250 gallons of water a day, compared with five gallons for the average African household—the equivalent of one toilet flush in the United States. But, as the world becomes more connected, even we may soon feel the pinch. By the year 2025, fully two-thirds of the world's population may be living with some amount of stress around water. '

The problem with water, though, is that the shortfalls don't show up until the very end. You can go on pumping unsustainably until the day you run out. Then all you have is the recharge flow, which comes from precipitation. This is not decades away, this is years away. We're already seeing huge shortages in China, where the Yellow River runs dry for part of each year. The Yellow River is the cradle of Chinese civilization. It first failed to reach the sea in 1972, and since 1985 it's run dry for part of each year. For 1997 it was dry for 226 days.

—LESTER BROWN, quoted in interview in *Audubon,* November-December, 1999

FACT

Engineers have indicated that the massive Ogallala Aquifer of the Great Plains—the world's largest underground supply of water—could be pumped out within forty years, leading the United States to secure new freshwater supplies from Canada.

TIP

If the saying, "Think Globally, Act Locally," ever applied to anything, it applies to our global water use. Commonsense reductions in personal water use—and a better understanding of the vast amounts of water used to create the things we take for granted: cars, computers, agriculture, nuclear power—could save massive amounts of freshwater around the world.

28

Letting Creativity Flow

It is estimated that one billion people around the world must walk fifteen minutes or more from their homes to get freshwater, then wait in extended lines to pump and fill containers to lug back. Recently, a group of those people decided there had to be a better way. Upon seeing their children enjoying a local merry-go-round, one enterprising South African community outfitted the merry-go-round with a special pump, so every time the children played, the water flowed. The idea worked so well that more than five hundred similar pumps are now in use throughout the country.

All over East Africa—indeed, all over Africa—it is normal for people to walk a kilometer or two or six for water. In more arid areas, people walk even greater distances, and sometimes all they find at the end is a pond slimy with overuse. More than ninety percent of Africans still dig for their water, and waterborne diseases such as typhoid, dysentery, bilharzia, and cholera are common. The bodies of many Africans are a stew of parasites. In some areas the wells are so far below the earth's surface that chains of people are required to pass up the water.

—MARQ DE VILLIERS, *Water*, 2000

Whose Water Is It, Anyway?

Almost 10 percent of the world's water systems are under the control of a private company, and that number is increasing rapidly. With corporate companies managing public water systems, this public resource is quickly becoming a private commodity. At the current rate, 70 percent of the water systems in Europe and North America may soon be owned and managed by private corporations.

Water is the most precious, limited natural resource we have in this country. . . . But because water belongs to no one—except the people—special interests, including government polluters, use it as their private sewers.

—RALPH NADER, quoted in *Water Wasteland* by David Zwick and Marcy Benstock, 1971

We must treat water as if it were the most precious thing in the world, the most valuable natural resource. Be economical with water! Don't waste it! We still have time to do something about this problem before it is too late.

—MIKHAIL GORBACHEV, president of Green Cross International

TIP

Remember, water should be considered a fundamental human right belonging to no one and not to be sold to the highest bidder. As they say, you can switch from Coke to Pepsi, but if you don't like the company that delivers your tap water, then where do you turn?

30

A Thirstier World

Not only are we drinking the same amount of water that was here at the creation of the planet, it's the same water the dinosaurs drank, bless their reptilian hearts. Fortunately, many of the dire population predictions that scared everyone in the 1970s have tapered down a little, but that doesn't mean the pressure on our resources is dwindling. The United Nations predicts that the current number of two billion people with poor or little access to freshwater will swell to five billion in less than twenty years.

Although our basic needs are the same for people all over the world, the amount of water we actually use in daily life differs enormously. In Africa, an average Masai family uses just over one gallon (four liters) of water per person, per day. In Los Angeles, an average family uses almost 130 gallons (five hundred liters) of water per person, per day.

—PETER SWANSON, *Water: The Drop of Life,* 2001

Multinational companies now run water systems for 7 percent of the world's population, and analysts say that figure could grow to 17 percent by 2015. Private water management is estimated to be a $200 billion business, and the World Bank, which has encouraged governments to sell off their utilities to reduce public debt, projects it could be worth $1 trillion by 2021. The potential for profits is staggering: In May 2000 *Fortune* magazine predicted that water is about to become "one of the world's great business opportunities," and that "it promises to be to the twenty-first century what oil was to the twentieth."

—JOHN LOUMA, "Water Thieves," *Ecologist,* March 2004

FACT

To accommodate growth in global population, experts believe that we must use every drop of water twice as well as we do now. Thanks to improved technologies such as drip irrigation, improvements in plumbing systems, and improved conservation communication programs, the ability to do this is at our fingertips.

31

Shouldn't I Know Something About the Greenhouse Effect?

Yes! You should. The greenhouse effect occurs when heat energy from sunlight becomes trapped by excess carbon dioxide and water vapor in the atmosphere. Instead of certain radiation, or heat energy, being reflected by the earth back into space, it bounces back to us, vaporizing our oceans, lakes, and rivers, in an ever-worsening cycle that scientists refer to as a feedback loop.

To a patient scientist, the unfolding greenhouse mystery is far more exciting than the plot of the best mystery novel. But it is slow reading, with new clues sometimes not appearing for several years. Impatience increases when one realizes that it is not the fate of some fictional character, but of our planet and species, which hangs in the balance as the great carbon mystery unfolds at a seemingly glacial pace.

—DAVID W. SCHINDLER, "The Mysterious Missing Sink," *Nature: 398* (1999)

FACT

A car rated at 32 miles per gallon driven fifteen thousand miles a year emits around two tons less CO_2 than a car that gets average gas mileage (about 22 mpg).

TIP

Automakers have gotten serious about vehicles with low carbon dioxide emissions. If your vehicle is barely meeting current EPA emissions standards, consider trading it in for any number of new, low-emission vehicles.

32

Grab Bag

With improvements in technology, the average consumer has many cost-effective options to reduce water consumption and do their part to keep our remaining water clean.

You don't have to be the head of a company to help a business change, and you don't have to be an elected official to help get the government to act. You just need a vision of what you're trying to accomplish, why it's important, and a clear sense of how to do it.

—THE EARTHWORKS GROUP, *The Next Step: 50 More Things You Can Do to Save the Earth,* 1991

FACT

Over the past twenty-five years, the state of Massachusetts has reduced water demands by 25 percent, with a "fix-it" program that includes aggressive leak repairs and the installation of efficient plumbing fixtures and devices.

A few effective water-saving options include:

- Low-flush toilets.
- Devices to catch roof water for use on gardens.
- Water-saving washing machines.
- Installing plumbing systems that reuse "gray water" from baths and showers for flushing toilets.
- Landscaping with plants that are adapted to the local climate.
- Support for local land-use ordinances that protect wetlands, aquifers, and watersheds.

33

Small Car,
Big Savings

This is the chapter you were afraid to see. Most of us love the luxury of a roomy car. Not only is it comfortable, but it's also a convenient way to shuttle the local Little League team from practice to pizza. But bigger cars often use more gas. And since it takes nearly five gallons of water to produce a quarter gallon of gas, if a smaller, more fuel-efficient car fits your lifestyle equally well, you might want to give that option some extra consideration.

There are two ways to get enough: One is to continue to accumulate more and more. The other is to desire less.

—G.K. CHESTERTON (1874-1936)

Gas prices continue to rise. At the gas station near my house they have a slot for your credit card and one right next to it for your 401(K).

—JAY LENO

FACT

Auto manufacturers have dramatically improved the efficiency of SUVs. But as of the publication of this book, the average SUV still consumes roughly twice as much gasoline per mile than standard cars. Or to put it another way: Switching from an average new car to a 13 mpg SUV for a year would waste more energy than leaving a refrigerator door open for six years.

Americans drive over one trillion miles a year.

TIP

This one's a no-brainer: Are you and your car the right fit? If not, maybe it's time to rethink your relationship.

BONUS TIP: Still not ready to trade in that SUV you love? Ease your guilt by slowing down. Driving at 50 mph uses 25 percent less fuel than 70 mph.

34

Fishometers

Can a fish tell temperature? You might think so given the amount of mercury in their bodies. As larger fish eat smaller critters that contain mercury, the mercury levels in their bodies build up. It can build up in your body, too. Eating fish that contain high levels of mercury on a regular basis can cause serious health problems—particularly for children and pregnant women. A recent Centers for Disease Control report estimates that 12 percent of U.S. women of childbearing age and up to 630,000 children born each year suffer from unsafe levels of mercury in their bodies. Some of the species with high mercury levels may surprise you. They include tuna, tilefish, swordfish, shark, king mackerel, and grouper.

With chemicals, it's shoot first and ask questions later.

—AL MEYERHOFF, coauthor of the Environmental Protection Initiative of 1990

Mercury gets into our water sources from coal-fired power plants, chlorine-alkali processing, waste incineration, and metal processing. Most of it is air pollution before it sinks into the waterways. Increasing levels of mercury contamination of North America's waterways have resulted in almost all U.S. states and most Canadian provinces issuing fish consumption advisories covering 30 percent of U.S. lakes (twelve million acres) and 453 thousand miles of America's rivers—with fish too contaminated with mercury for safe consumption by many members of our communities.

Know what you are eating. The National Resource Defense Council has listings of fish consumption advisories across the United States. If you want to stop the mercury problems at the source, lend your support to watchdog groups, such as the U.S. Waterkeeper Alliance, that ensure that companies are meeting emissions laws.

35

Breeding Goodwill

What do you buy for the person who has everything? May we suggest a cow, a llama, and silkworms? Now before you run over to the local petting zoo, we should probably clarify that these are gifts *on behalf* of your privileged friends—and they would benefit a family far, far away.

Innovation is the ability to see change as an opportunity— not a threat.

—Anonymous

FACT

A cleaner environment is often tied to a healthier economy. If dynamite blasting a coral reef is the only way to earn enough money to feed a family in an underdeveloped nation, the reef will always lose. Groups like Heifer International, however, provide solutions that help people preserve natural resources and still feed their families. They teach villages about breeding livestock and sustainable practices— and even throw in the cows, which in turn bring milk, meat, fertilizer, and cash to the village. As the cows produce more cows, the villagers share their lessons and cows with other villages. Depending on what is appropriate to the region, Heifer International will even provide rabbits, chickens, and silkworms.

TIP

Understand that, like seven degrees of separation, some of the best environmental practices take several steps. (And . . . we really like the idea of giving your Uncle George in Miami a llama.)

Part III

Go with the Flow

36

Welcome to
Disposable Island

"**N**OW AVAILABLE: Texas-sized island in the Northern Pacific. Free for the taking." Sounds pretty good, right? Not if you read the fine print and discover the island in question is made of nothing but trash. According to scientists, our oceans harbor massive amounts of plastic trash that will never go away.

I have always been a big advocate of tap water—not because I think it's harmless but because the idea of purchasing water extracted from some remote watershed and then hauled halfway round the world bothers me. Drinking bottled water relieves people of their concern about ecological threats to the river they live by or to the basins of groundwater they live over. It's the same kind of thinking that leads some to the complacent conclusion that if things on earth get bad enough, well, we'll just blast off to a space station somewhere else.

—SANDRA STEINGRABER,
Having Faith, 2001

It's time we started thinking of plastics as permanent instead of disposable. Otherwise, we could be looking at new business opportunities to build homes on trash islands. We know we asked already, but please recycle your plastics and buy things with less plastic packaging.

Most plastics photodegrade, not biodegrade. That means that sunlight *sloooowly* breaks them into smaller and smaller pieces of plastic polymers. The problem is that bacteria can't break down these plastic polymers. The ocean is now becoming a plastic polymer and plankton soup, and what we are seeing today is the result of plastics from the 1950s that have had a chance to photodegrade.

An on-the-go society combined with masses of health-conscious consumers has turned the single-serve bottle of water into a national icon. According to the California Department of Conservation, more than one billion water bottles are winding up in the trash in California each year. That translates into nearly three million empty water bottles going to the trash *every* day and an estimated $26 million in unclaimed California Refund Value deposits annually. If recycled, the raw materials from those bottles could be used to make 74 million square feet of carpet, 74 million extra large T-shirts or 16 million sweaters, among other things.

37

A Stranger in Your Tank

Fish tanks are gorgeous. They make great stress relievers. They can even be educational. But there lurks a darker side to your tank—you may want to start running background checks on your fish. Do you know where they came from? How they got here?

Many fish that end up for sale have quite a history. Chances are they were collected with dubious techniques: cyanide squirted into the water to drug them, dynamite blasting to temporarily knock them out, illegal collecting in places where the fish are endangered. Most of the fish are so stressed they don't even make it to the store.

This may sound very cloak and dagger, but there is something you can do—purchase aquarium fish from Marine Aquarium Council certified fish stores and dealers. They check to make sure the fish they buy and sell have been collected legally and in environmentally friendly ways. Those fish are also more likely to survive once you get them home. Or go one step further to purchase fish that have been tank bred and raised so you aren't removing any from their natural home.

38

Make Your House a Home

Many people are taking conservation into their own hands—and they're doing it in an unexpected way. Tired of sit-ins, protests, and marches, these former radicals—many of whom have shed their old ways to become CEOs and business leaders—are taking quiet action by simply making a sanctuary in their own backyards. You can do the same. You can help our beautiful blue planet with some small-scale habitat restoration at home. Wildflower meadows, mini-orchards, and heirloom vegetables not only give your home a trendy wildness, they'll help turn your suburban nest into a haven for environmental sanity.

To me a lush carpet of pine needles or spongy grass is more welcome than the most luxurious Persian rug.

—HELEN KELLER (1880-1968)

What is a weed? A plant whose virtues have not yet been discovered.

—RALPH WALDO EMERSON (1803-1882), *Fortune of the Republic,* 1878

TIP

Ever wonder why we see fewer and fewer of our eastern and western bluebirds? These animals don't compete well with aliens like starlings. A natural remedy like a shallow pool of fresh water for a birdbath can give these birds a chance at a new start.

39

Smart Dinner Talk

You are at a seafood restaurant—you love seafood. Hey, most people do and it can be a healthy part of your diet. But lately you've been hearing rumors: This or that fish is endangered, or the shrimp were caught in some weird, destructive way. Your date is into protecting the environment and she probably knows all about this stuff. No sweat! The solution to your dilemma is here! There is a Web site (http://www.seafoodwatch.org) that tells you if your favorite seafood is endangered or sustainable, or fished in an environmentally friendly way. You can even print out a little card that fits in your wallet for easy reference (impress the girl, *and* help save the oceans—not a bad date).

Since 1988, when the world's seafood supply peaked at thirty-four pounds a person each year, the combined effects of overfishing and increasing human populations have reduced the amount of fish and shellfish available on Earth to only about twenty-five pounds a person each year, according to the findings. And this trend is projected to continue rapidly downward to less than seventeen pounds a person each year by 2020.

—"China, U.N. Challenged Over Fish," MSNBC.com, November 28, 2001

Fully 90 percent of each of the world's large ocean species, including cod, halibut, tuna, swordfish, and marlin, has disappeared from the world's oceans in recent decades, according to the Canadian analysis—the first to use historical data dating to the beginning of large-scale fishing, in the 1950s. The new research found that fishing has become so efficient that it typically takes just fifteen years to remove 80 percent or more of any species that becomes the focus of a fleet's attention. Some populations have disappeared within just a few years, belying the oceans' reputation as a refuge and resource of nearly infinite proportions.

—RICK WEISS, "Key Ocean Fish Species Ravaged, Study Finds," *Washington Post,* May 15, 2003

FACT

We have better technology, more people, and more boats than ever before. We are taking some fish species out of the ocean faster than they can reproduce.

TIP

What will you find at seafoodwatch.org? Here's a little example: As much as nine pounds of other animals and fish get caught and wasted for every one pound of trawled shrimp. Trawling means dragging a net with heavy weights across the ocean floor, mowing down everything in its path—like clear-cutting an enormous patch of rainforest. Try trapped shrimp instead of trawled shrimp—doesn't hurt the habitat and doesn't catch other critters.

Not long ago, I ventured into the Sea of Cortez with a group of local fishermen. These people knew the waters well, and I asked them to take our team of SCUBA divers to a reef known for its abundance of hammerhead sharks. Unfortunately, when we arrived at the reef, the sharks were noticeably absent. While this might be a welcome sight to many people, for me the tragedy was all too obvious. Without the sharks, the entire ecosystem had been thrown off balance, and the reef had slipped into decline. "What happened?" I asked the fishermen. I quickly learned the effects—and painful reality—of long-lining—the practice of stretching a monofilament line as far as sixty miles with thousands of baited hooks. The United States National Oceanographic and Atmospheric Agency reports that shallow longline fishing captures and kills 4.4 million sharks, seabirds, billfish, marine mammals, and sea turtles each year in the Pacific Ocean. This is especially bad news for the sharks, whose numbers have declined by as much as 90 percent in the Atlantic and Gulf of Mexico. It has turned out that a lucrative demand for shark fin soup in Asia has hit shark fisheries hard. Even if the sharks are released, without their fins they are left to die a slow, painful death. Moreover, without the sharks, the entire ecosystem breaks down, including the coral reefs—all for a dish that is the equivalent of fingernails boiled in water.

—Wyland

40

Watered-Down Techno Trash

Once upon a time, in the antediluvian 1980s, electronics were so expensive and technology developed so slowly that people kept things like television sets, stereos, and computers for ten years or more. Nowadays, technology is changing so quickly that the cell phone you bought last month with picture and video capability now comes with TV on it, too—and, well, we've gotta have it. While our devices aren't broken, their useful life (to some of us) is short.

FACT

- In the next three years, individuals and organizations worldwide will replace more than four hundred million computers. This will generate more than four billion pounds of plastic, one billion pounds of lead waste, and millions of pounds of other toxic materials, including arsenic and cadmium.
- The average cell phone in the United States is replaced after just eighteen months.
- More than 75 percent of all computers ever sold remain stockpiled in our closets, garages, office storage rooms, and warehouses.

Batteries that end up in landfills and incinerators eventually leak into the environment and end up in the food chain, causing serious health risks to humans and animals. Congress got wise to some of these problems in 1996, when it signed the Battery Act into law. The law phased out the use of mercury in batteries and provided new collection methods and the proper disposal of batteries.

TIP

Don't throw your old electronics devices in the trash—these items contain toxins and elements harmful to the environment, fill the dumps, and could still be useful to someone. Sell your old equipment or donate it to a charity, or if it is beyond repair, it can be recycled. There are lists of agencies that will take the equipment off your hands. At http://www.earth911.org you can type in your zip code and find out who can recycle electronics in your area. Goodwill takes Pentium II computers and higher and uses them to provide job training. Cell phone service providers will take your used phone and give them or the profits to a variety of causes: battered women, the Keep America Beautiful campaign, or organizations that teach life skills to challenged people. Each company has its own charity that benefits from the donation of your cell phone, and you get a tax write-off!

A lot is riding on the success of the Electronic Waste Recycling Act, signed into law by Gov. Arnold Schwarzenegger in September 2003. The legislation was the first in the nation to attack the scourge of toxic e-waste piling up in America's garages and landfills. More than three thousand tons of electronics are discarded daily in the United States, and fifty million computers become obsolete every year, according to the U.S. Environmental Protection Agency.

—KARL SCHOENBERGER, "California's E-Waste Recycling Program Hits Stride," *San Jose Mercury News*, July 19, 2005

TIP

Switch to an LCD monitor; its environmental costs are comparable to CRTs, but it consumes much less power, and its parts are less harmful when disassembled. Talk to your hazardous materials recycler about where e-waste goes once you drop it off.

BONUS TIP: Americans use 2 to 5 billion batteries every year, which is great around the holidays when you want to play with that new square-dancing robot your boss gave you. But most batteries are not biodegradable, and they contain toxic heavy metals that could leak into landfills. Rechargeable batteries, on the other hand, can replace between fifty and three hundred throwaway batteries.

41

The Trouble with MTBE

A few years ago, gas companies agreed to government clean air laws by removing lead—a popular octane enhancer—from their fuels. Their solution was MTBE, or methyl tertiary-butyl ether, a fuel additive that juiced up the oxygen levels of gas, reduced knocks, and cut back on carbon monoxide. MTBE was cheap, easy to produce, and helped gasoline burn more completely, reducing tailpipe emissions. Everything seemed great until it was realized that MTBE, a suspected carcinogen, was becoming increasingly linked to contaminated groundwater.

In the News

The Energy Policy Act of 2005, signed by President Bush in August, requires 7.5 billion gallons of ethanol and biodiesel to enter the nation's fuel supply by 2012, providing 5.75 percent of the nation's transportation-fuel needs.

From Tank of Gas to Drinking Glass . . .

An underground storage tank (UST) may take years to rust; it probably won't begin leaking until long after the people who bought it and installed it have left their jobs. Even after it begins to leak, it may take several more years before appreciable concentrations of chemicals appear in the aquifer—and it will likely be years beyond that before any health effects show up. So it's quite possible that any cancers occurring today as a result of leaking USTs might originate from tanks that were installed half a century ago.

—PAYAL SAMPAT, "Groundwater Shock," *World Watch*, January–February 2000

FACT

As of 2004, more than half of all states in America still permitted the use of MTBE.

Analysts believe the cost of cleaning up all MTBE in the United States could run as high as $140 billion, including breaking down the compound in municipal water supplies and repairing leaky underground oil tanks.

TIP

Support the use of fuels containing ethanol, a gasoline additive derived mainly from corn, instead of MTBE. Although some critics point to the high energy costs associated with corn farming and environmental impacts such as fertilizer pollution, ethanol helps fuel burn cleanly and does not pollute the air or water like MTBE.

42

Hooked On Dry-Cleaning

It ain't no mountain stream, but it beats the alternative. A new organic dry cleaner claims that its organic dry-cleaning process is so environmentally friendly that tests included trout actually swimming—no, thriving—in its wastewater. We won't name the brand, but we applaud the effort. Over the years, the cleaning solvent of choice for dry cleaners was perchloroethylene (PERC), a pungent water and air pollutant and possible carcinogen. Effects of short-term exposure to PERC could range from dizziness, fatigue, headaches, and sweating to lack of coordination and unconsciousness. Long-term exposure could cause liver and kidney damage.

And So . . .

After years of cleaning clothing with perchloroethylene, dry cleaners are using new methods like special detergents that dissolve in liquid carbon dioxide—a solution just like the CO_2 used to carbonate sodas. The process is environmentally friendly and reduces the health risks associated with traditional dry-cleaning solvents. (Although we still wonder whatever happened to those trout.)

I n summer 2002, the people of Bourne, Massachusetts, closed three of the town's six drinking water wells when it was discovered that the wells were contaminated with perchlorate, a rocket-fuel component that leaked from a nearby military reservation.

If It Was Good Enough for Thomas Jefferson

On the part of the open area surrounding the main house at Monticello that wasn't planted with all those vegetables, Thomas Jefferson decided not to put in the sweeping lawns that the owners of neighboring plantations favored to imitate European aristocracy. He maintained a variety of native meadow habitats and kept growth in check by tethering sheep nearby. If we accept Jefferson as our model in home horticulture as in so much else that makes us what we are, his precedent brands today's solid sod lawns as positively un-American.

Only in water and land blessed North America has a detached home surrounded by lawn become the standard dwelling. Since we suburbanized following the big wars, any land that wasn't cleared of native vegetation for farming, eliminating the furry little native mammals, bugs, and birds that once thrived there, was cleared to be wasted in acre after acre of short-trimmed grass suitable only for growing Japanese Beetle grubs and for frustrating lawn-mowing dads. May we offer a modest proposal? Let's require lawn permits, with a hefty fee to be charged for any home turf area much bigger than a badminton court or croquet field or maybe both, or maybe a football field or a baseball diamond if it's a really big family. Proceeds would be used to preserve threatened native habitats.

Before Tiger Woods came along, I'd have suggested imposing such a fee on private golf courses as well.

—JOHN VIVIAN, "Growing Wild: Take Your Home Place (Almost) All the Way Back to Nature," *Mother Earth News*, December 1, 1997

43

Wild, Wonderful Wetlands

They say that beauty is in the eye of the beholder. And while mangroves, swamps, marshes, and bogs might not be as aesthetically pleasing to some people as a green valley in Yosemite, these natural filters are one of the most effective ways of controlling pollutants that choke our waters. They store floodwaters, convert toxic pollutants through biochemical processes to less harmful substances, stabilize shorelines, and act as spawning or nursery grounds for about two-thirds of our commercial fish.

The real conflict of the beach is not between sea and shore, for theirs is only a lover's quarrel, but between man and nature. On the beach, nature has achieved a dynamic equilibrium that is alien to man and his static sense of equilibrium. Once a line has been established, whether it be a shoreline or a property line, man unreasonably expects it to stay put.

—G. SOUCIE, *Smithsonian,* 1973

T I P

Once destroyed, regaining a full-fledged, viable wetland is not easy. Restoring the delicate balance of native species is expensive and laborious. However, scientists and economists are discovering that the costs of species destruction, flooding, and disease caused by destroyed wetlands may outweigh the benefits of a coastal housing tract, fish farm, or harbor. Flooding from wetlands destruction costs billions of dollars, yet state and federal agencies gave developers 99 percent of the wetland destruction permits requested between 1988 and 1996, even in high-flood states like Texas, California, Ohio, Missouri, and Illinois, the sites of the country's worst flood disasters.

FACT

An estimated 95 percent of commercial fish and 85 percent of sport fish spend a portion of their lives in coastal wetlands. Yet wetlands continue to be subject to near relentless draining, dredging, and filling. Three hundred years ago, an estimated 221 million acres existed in the regions that are now the lower forty-eight states. Today, more than half of those wetlands have disappeared. In California alone, 90 percent of all wetlands have been destroyed.

Wetlands occur in every country and in every climatic zone, and are considered among the world's most important environmental assets. An acre of wetlands can store up to 1.6 million gallons of floodwater, according to researchers, depending on the type of wetland. Prairie pothole wetlands can store more. Restoring prairie potholes and wetlands can reduce hundred-year floods by up to 40 percent, according to USDA studies.

11

Power of the Pen

A lot of water goes in to making paper. Fortunately, you can put that paper to good use by sending it directly to your local representative to advocate for smarter water-usage policies. Representatives pay close attention to the mail they receive, and they believe that one letter equates to the opinions of about one hundred people. By organizing a letter or e-mail writing campaign to a member of Congress or a particular government agency, you can greatly impact the way a legislator votes on a particular issue.

Here are a few ideas to make your letter writing campaign even more successful:

1. Always start your letter with a proper title, e.g., Honorable Representative;
2. Make sure your letter reaches your representative with enough time for the representative to consider taking action;
3. Be specific about the legislative proposal or issue you are writing about and explain what you want them to do;
4. Stick to one or two key issues;
5. Include your address on your letter, as well as on the envelope. Most congressional offices respond to mail only from their districts or areas;
6. Use supporting facts to strengthen your point;
7. The United States House of Representatives Web site has the names, addresses, and e-mail addresses for every representative. Visit the site at http://www.house.gov/writerep/;
8. Find your senator's contact information at http://www.senate.gov/general/contact_information/senators_cfm.cfm.

For a sample advocacy letter, see Appendix 6.

FACT

In spring of 1978, residents of Love Canal, a neighborhood in Niagara Falls, New York, discovered that a dump site containing twenty thousand tons of chemical wastes, including DDT, heavy metals, PCBs, and multiple solvents, was leaking into their neighborhood. With illnesses running rampant in the community, the Love Canal Homeowners Association—none of whom were political activists—went to work on one of the most successful community activism campaigns in history. By putting pressure on elected officials, giving hundreds of news media interviews, writing letters, and circulating petitions, the group influenced the passage of the Superfund law of 1980, which requires the companies responsible to ultimately fund the cleanup of toxic waste sites.

BONUS TIP: So you've read the papers, heard both sides of an issue, and you've decided to give your local representative a piece of your mind. But why not see how they think in the first place? Many Web sites, including http://www.citizen.org, can tell you how legislators voted on environmental issues.

Watchdog for Water

Several decades ago, wholesale dumping of waste into our water systems was not uncommon. Fortunately, community outcry and legislative action called for tougher controls on water pollution from industries and sewage treatment plants. But problems remain when nonpoint source pollution such as pesticides, grease, oils, toxic chemicals, and heavy metals from farms, homes, automobiles, and other sources are picked up from rainfall, snowmelt, and irrigation and deposited into rivers, lakes, coastal waters, and our own groundwater.

FACT: The United States has roughly fifty-five thousand community water systems, all of which must test their water and treat it before distributing to customers.

BUT: In developing countries, on average, 90 to 95 percent of all domestic sewage and 75 percent of all industrial waste goes straight into lakes and rivers without any treatment whatsoever.

FACT

According to the U.S. Environmental Protection Agency, nonpoint source pollution is the main reason that approximately 40 percent of our rivers, lakes, and estuaries are not clean enough to meet basic uses such as fishing or swimming.

TIP

Water can often look extremely clean, but sometimes looks can be deceiving. If you really want to roll up your sleeves and be a watchdog for clean water in your community, a group called the Global Rivers Environmental Education Network has designed a Web site with resources you can use to implement a local water monitoring program and store, share, and compare your data with others in your area. To get started, visit http://www.green.org or visit the EPA's "Surf Your Watershed" Web site at http://www.epa.gov/surf/ for more information.

Part IV

A Global View

46

Unsafe Water: The Human Cost

The World Health Organization estimates that 1.8 million people die every year because of diarrhea; 90 percent are children under five years old, and 88 percent of those cases result from bad water and sanitation. In sub-Saharan Africa, about 280 million people drink water from unprotected wells, springs, and surface water sources laden with malaria and intestinal worms. Even in urban areas, nearly one-quarter of households get water from unprotected sources. To remedy this, United Nations members pledged in 2000 to halve the number of people lacking access to clean water by 2015 by drilling communal boreholes fitted with hand pumps or standpipes to access protected underground water.

FACT: With a typical annual income of less than $100 per person, it is nearly impossible for a small village in South Africa's Eastern Cape Province to maintain a standpipe that costs $230 per person to install and $25 per household to run.

TIP

As a United States citizen you have a say in how the federal government spends its money—at home and abroad. In the book, Blue Gold, authors Maude Barlow and Tony Clarke believe the United States should not support the policies of any international financing organization, such as the World Bank or the International Monetary Fund, that would result in poor people losing access to clean drinking water. At the very least, the authors say, any water privatization plan must include a water lifeline for every citizen.

FACT

The EPA estimates that Americans spend only seven-tenths of 1 percent of U.S. household median income on their water bill—a rate that experts believe is far too low to cover long-run costs.

Proposed water privatization and "total cost recovery" plans may have short-term benefits for governments—but the expense to the poor can be catastrophic. In 2002, researchers in the KwaZulu-Natal province of South Africa linked a wide-spread cholera outbreak to the government's decision to replace free community standpipes with pre-paid water meters. The conversion was the equivalent of a water cutoff for hundreds of thousands of people, who were forced to decrease their consumption of water, or draw water from contaminated rivers and streams. After the installation of the meters, more than 110,000 people were infected with cholera.

A Head Start on Innovation

To recoin an old phrase: Maybe youth isn't wasted on the young, after all. Case in point: A group of South African students put their heads together in 2005 to help relieve their drought-plagued nation of water waste. Pontso Moletsane, Motobele Motshodi, and Sechaba Ramabenyane used light sensors to control water pipe valves in their town, so automatic irrigation would occur mostly at night. By automating irrigation this way, less water would be lost to evaporation. The invention was technically simple and inexpensive to produce. Yet it enabled communities to use limited water resources more efficiently to improve food production and to improve poverty conditions. All it took was an interest in science—and their community.

Inanimate objects are sometimes parties to litigation. A ship has legal personality. . . . The corporation . . . is an acceptable adversary and large fortunes ride on its cases...So it should be as respects valleys, ridges, groves of trees, swampland, or even air that feels the destructive pressures of modern technology and modern life. The river, for example, is the living symbol of all the life it sustains or nourishes—fish, aquatic insects, water ouzels, otter, fisher, deer, elk, bear, and all other animals, including man, who are dependent on it or who enjoy it for its sight, its sound, or its life. The river as plaintiff speaks for the ecological unit of life that is part of it.

—Justice WILLIAM O. DOUGLAS (1898-1980), dissenting opinion, Supreme Court of the United States, No. 70-34, *Sierra Club v. Morton*, 1972

FACT

According to a November 2001 U.S. Department of Education report, seven out of ten fourth- and eighth-graders in the United States could not grasp the scientific knowledge and skills necessary to do challenging work for their grade levels, and twelfth-graders were doing worse in science than their twelfth-grade predecessors five years earlier.

TIP

Here's an easy one. Encourage local school districts to hire more teachers who have been trained in science—and support curriculum that calls for increased science teaching. The students these teachers educate will hold the future of our planet in their hands.

BONUS TIP: Give tomorrow's scientists and teachers even more of a head start. Lend your support to organizations and programs such as the JASON Project, Project Wet, and the Wyland Ocean Challenge that supplement classroom science and environmental education.

48

People, People Everywhere—and Only So Many Drops to Drink

New concerns over the future of available freshwater have led researchers to take a tough look at population growth. In 1998, thirty-one countries, accounting for 8 percent of the world population, faced chronic freshwater shortages. Projections indicate that unless new strategies are enacted, more than 2.8 billion people—about 35 percent of the world's projected population—could run short of water.

Ask a person in New York what he thinks about the water problem and he will probably say, "What problem?" Ask a person in New Delhi and you will be lucky if you escape with a fifteen-minute lecture on how the water flows once a day, it has to be stored, it smells and, if you drink it without boiling it, chances are you will get sick.

—ASHALI VARMA, "Will water soon be too expensive for the poor of the world?," *Earth Times News,* May 4, 1998

It isn't pollution that's harming the environment. It's the impurities in our air and water that are doing it.

—Former U.S. Vice President DAN QUAYLE

FACT

Pollution plays an equal if not greater role in availability of freshwater than the amount of resources on hand. Malaria, cholera, and typhoid are present in water systems with improper waste disposal and poor management. Even if countries like Ethiopia, India, Kenya, and Peru have abundant water, high levels of pollution can easily bring about an availability crisis.

TIP

Experts say there is no more water on earth now than there was two thousand years ago when the population of our planet was less than 3 percent of its current size. Okay, so maybe we've grown a little bit since then. But, in addition to better water management and water treatment methods, you can help ensure a sustainable level of population in relation to the supply of freshwater by supporting family planning programs around the world.

49

Vanishing Act

Imagine a lake roughly the size of Vermont. That's how big Lake Chad was in the 1960s. Once among the largest freshwater lakes in Africa, the lake has shrunk from nearly ten thousand square miles to only 839 miles—nearly one-twentieth of its size—over the last forty years. Some of this shrinkage comes from natural climate changes. But many scientists today attribute most of the shrinking of Lake Chad to increasing demands for water by the country of Chad itself and its drought-plagued neighbors Nigeria, Niger, and Cameroon.

Today, irrigation accounts for two-thirds of global water use. And lakes aren't the only victims. The inland Aral Sea in central Asia, for example, has suffered unprecedented depletion as the two rivers that feed it, the Amu Darya and the Syr Darya, yield their water to crop irrigation. Once the fourth largest inland body of water in the world, the

Aral has lost four-fifths of its volume since the early 1960s, splitting into two sections and altering the climate and livelihood for millions of people.

T he Black Sea is spiraling into decline as a result of chronic overfishing, high levels of pollution, and the devastating impacts of alien species, an international team of scientists has warned. . . . The findings have come from a regional team who are members of the Global International Waters Assessment (GIWA), an initiative led by the United Nations Environment Programme (UNEP). . . . The environment, wildlife, and people linked with the Black Sea are also under threat from large discharges of raw sewage, damaging levels of coastal erosion, and the suffocating impacts of dumping of sludges and muds dredged from ports, the GIWA scientists said. . . . "We have known for some time that the Black Sea, a water system of global importance, has been suffering, but these results bring into sharp focus just how damaged it is and the risks to the millions of people who depend upon it for food and livelihoods. The findings are a warning to the world that we cannot take the health of our water systems for granted."

—"International Team Combats Black Sea Decline," Environment News Service, October 10, 2001

FACT

In order to support burgeoning populations, the demand on many of the world's largest lakes has exceeded the available supply. Lake Chapala, the largest lake in Mexico, has lost more than 80 percent of its water since the 1970s due to increased agricultural demand.

OUTLOOK: The problems of the Aral Sea—and vanishing lakes—have been closely monitored by international organizations. The future of these bodies now depends on the cooperation of upstream and downstream governmental organizations through market reform, interstate water cooperation, and stabilizing declining environments.

TIP

Protect natural lakes—and lake basins—even if no water remains in them. One of the reasons for increasing water scarcity is that dried lake areas are increasingly reclaimed for farming, businesses, and homes. With such a blur of development, researchers can no longer determine the original boundaries of the lakes and lack the ability to properly evaluate the impact of the loss—studies that could lead to better urban planning, and even hope for reviving the lakes.

50

Where's Your Next Drink Coming From?

If you thought your next drink might be your last, you'd probably want to take a big gulp. Or better yet, you'd simply hoard as much as humanly possible. This condition of "unknowing" has led to huge and often unnecessary reductions of available freshwater in regions where people are uncertain of the future flow.

As the number of international river basins (and impact of water scarcity) has grown so do the warnings that countries will take up arms to ensure their access to water. In 1995, for example, World Bank vice president Ismail Serageldin claimed "the wars of the next century will be about water." These apocalyptic warnings fly in the face of history: No nations have gone to war specifically over water resources for thousands of years. International water disputes—even among fierce enemies—are resolved peacefully, even as conflicts erupt over other issues. In fact, instances of cooperation between riparian nations outnumbered conflicts by more than two to one between 1945 and 1999. Why? Because water is so important, nations cannot afford to fight over it.

—AARON T. WOLF, ANNIKA KRAMER, ALEXANDER CARIUS, and GEOFFREY D. DABELKO. "Water Can Be a Pathway to Peace, Not War." WorldWatch Insitute, Letter to the Global Policy Forum, June 2005

Governments that give people a better sense of how much water they'll have in the future—and fully share how that water is allocated—can reduce hoarding. Even a better understanding of the unpredictability of available freshwater can help people everywhere use water more wisely—and save lives.

FACT

Nearly one hundred countries share just thirteen major rivers and lakes. More than two hundred rivers systems cross international borders. With growing populations competing for resources, conflicts can arise. Yet, countries have shown the ability to successfully negotiate and agree over this tricky issue—a vital first step to improving shared water use.

In 1999, two farmers in Thailand were shot over a water dispute. Police said that both men had diverted water from a canal into their own irrigation channels in anticipation of a summer drought.

BONUS TIP: Support international policies and treaties that include water peacemaking strategies, which can create shared regional identities and cooperation on issues larger than water. Take for example, Israel and Jordan, which held secret "picnic table" talks to manage the Jordan River since 1953, even though they were officially at war from 1948 until the 1994 treaty.

51

Are You Retaining Enough Water?

Nature's miraculous powers of adaptation have much to teach us. Over the course of time, in the harshest of conditions, nature has found a way to survive. In poor light, owls have developed keen sight, while bats use echolocation to make their way through damp caves. In the desert, animals have adapted to diffuse heat with body temperatures that fluctuate with the temperature of the surrounding environment and hang on to the relatively small amounts of water at hand through a variety of ways.

So much water is pumped in and out of underground aquifers in the Los Angeles area that much of the landscape rises and falls more than four inches each year. . . . The immense annual groundswell caused by pumping practices is one hundred times larger than normal seismic fluctuations. It is particularly notable in northern parts of Orange County, where 75 percent of all the water used is pumped from the ground. The ground movement overshadows the more subtle tectonic forces at work along Southern California's countless thrust faults. ". . .It is actually quite astonishing," said geophysicist Gerald Bawden at the U.S. Geological Survey in Menlo Park, who led the study team. "The magnitude and extent of these motions are a product of Los Angeles' great thirst for water; they are unprecedented, and have not been observed elsewhere in the world." The new data—representing the first time the seasonal cycle has been measured—are reported today in the journal *Nature*. From fall to early spring, officials pump water into underground aquifers for storage, causing the land to rise. In summer months, these unseen reservoirs slowly collapse, systematically drained to water lawns, wash cars, top off swimming pools and slake the thirst of the area's four-teen million residents. Overall, the level of the water table sinks lower each year, leaving a permanent imprint on the land.

—ROBERT LEE HOTZ and KENNETH REICH, "Aquifer Levels May Lift, Lower L.A. Land," *Los Angeles Times,* August 23, 2001

FACT

The kangaroo rat obtains all its water from food, and it is among the world's most efficient mammals at conserving and recycling moisture. The Joshua tree of the Mojave Desert (*Yucca brevifolia*) has spongy, shallow roots to take advantage of even the smallest amounts of rain and has plant tissues that store large amounts of water for later use.

In the United States, each of us has the power to coexist with nature by recognizing the realities of our environment. Dry climates require greater adaptation to use available water resources efficiently. Wet climates are easily taken for granted, and their great abundance of water is often overused, misallocated, and polluted. Now, more and more people are returning long-banished native plants to their yards, from cactuses and yuccas in the West, to buffalo grass in the high plains and live oak and buttonwood in Florida. In Atlanta, where home lawn demands have drained water resources, hundreds of homeowners have ripped up their lawns and replaced them with backyard wildlife patches certified by the National Wildlife Federation. These people have done it—and so can you.

BONUS TIP: There are an estimated twenty million acres of lawns in the United States. On average, each acre requires more than twenty-seven thousand gallons of water every week. If you have to keep your lawn, set your automated sprinkler to go on in the early morning. This will help reduce the amount of water needed as water evaporates four to eight times faster in the heat of midday than it does in the morning.

52

A Big Dip
in the Great Lakes

Wait a second, you say. There's water everywhere. Huge reservoirs,
lakes, rivers. Moving a little here and there isn't going to hurt. That's
precisely what a shipping company thought when it obtained a permit
from the Ontario Ministry of the Environment to take 159 million gallons of water a year from Lake Superior for five years. In spring 1998,
the ship floated out from Sault Ste. Marie, Michigan, into the lake,
opened its hold, and took in water to be sold later to investors in Asia.
Futurists have heralded it as the first volley in the future of a world
water war.

The Great Lakes Basin contains one-fifth of the world's freshwater supply. As aquifers empty and droughts occur, futurists believe that the abundance of water in the Great Lakes—and similar water basins—could become a source of international tension.

In 2001, Nestlé, the world's number-one drinking water company, began bottling water drawn from ground wells surrounding the Great Lakes. The Swiss conglomerate holds a one-third share of the growing $7 billion-a-year market in bottled water.

Like oil reserves, the Great Lakes seem to provide an ideal solution to water shortages throughout the Southwest, and elsewhere around the world. They make a tempting solution, as local reservoirs dry and consumption grows, but this is a short-term—and shortsighted—solution. Conservation and awareness are still the best answers for pending water shortfalls.

Here in the Great Lakes region, a fourth year in a row of declining water levels has caused millions of dollars in losses for shipping companies, marinas, and other businesses and prompted further restrictions on future water withdrawals for expanding suburbs. "A lot of people just can't believe that we may be running out of water, living this close to the Great Lakes," said Sarah Nerenberg, a water engineer with the Northeastern Illinois Planning Commission, which conducted the study on shortages.

—TIMOTHY EFGAN, "Near Vast Bodies of Water, Land Lies Parched," *New York Times,* August 12, 2001

53

Debt for Nature

They may seem like separate issues, but poverty in third-world nations has a direct impact on our planet's environment, from depleted fisheries to deforestation to climate change. The greater a developing nation's debt, the more likely it is to practice unsustainable development. In some cases, groups like the Nature Conservancy, World Wildlife Fund, and Conservation International will relieve a portion of a less-developed country's foreign debt. In exchange, the country may agree to preserve a tract of land or water habitat. These "debt for nature" swaps have resulted in the preservation of tropical forests and saved the habitats of many species.

In his book *Debt and the Environment: Converging Crisis,* economist Morris Miller asserts that debt crisis is a significant factor in the deterioration of the environment in developing nations. While there are other causes, of course, debt for nature swaps may delay the destruction of habitats in time for alternative, innovative solutions.

TIP

Many third world nations have no option but to cash in on their natural resources—stripping rainforests, overfishing, and improperly dumping toxic waste—to keep up with interest payment on foreign debt. It's not a pretty picture. But you can be part of the global solution by investing in companies with positive environmental positions. Many corporations are indirectly involved in debt-for-nature swaps through their support of environmental groups. Financial institutions such as American Express and others have donated millions of dollars that have helped protect rainforests and reduced overharvesting.

Total debts amassed by the world's poorest countries shot up from $45 billion in 1970 to $934 billion in 2002, resulting in endless misery and widespread poverty as many of these economies spiraled out of control. In 1970, Africa's proportion of the total stood at less than $20 billion, not even half of the total owed by poor nations. By 2002, that had risen to well over half, or $527 billion. . . . And yet—despite having paid back $983 billion in principal and interest over the last three decades, on $965 billion of loans—they still go on paying, sacrificing both the health and the education of their people, as well as any prospect of economic recovery and growth.

—JORN MADSLIEN, "Debt Relief Hopes Bring Out the Critics," BBC News Online.
June 29, 2005

For a lesson in how quickly ecosystems fragment across international borders, a report today suggests looking no further than Lake Victoria. Prior to 1970, Lake Victoria, the world's largest tropical lake, had more than 350 species of fish from the cichlid family. Ninety percent of these were unique to the lake. The introduction of Nile perch and tilapia caused a collapse in the lake's biodiversity and deforestation in the three countries that border the lake, Uganda, Tanzania, and Kenya. Wood is needed to dry the oily perch, compared with the cichlids, which could be air-dried. Forest clearing has increased siltation and eutrophication in the lake, jeopardizing the Nile perch and tilapia fishery—the cause of the problem to begin with.

—"Lake Victoria Battles Biodiversity Breakdown," Environmental News Service,
December 1, 2000

54

Buy More! Save Less?

Call it affluenza, consumer madness, or keeping up with the Joneses. But the United States has built a foundation on more, bigger, better. While we can't fault anyone's aspirations for a better life, we can point out that this never-ending quest could one day reach a point of diminishing returns. And for that we blame—who else?—advertising. Well, okay, not entirely. But modern American advertising has reinforced our "culture of waste" to the point that we buy more and save less than any society in history. And, if you're wondering what all this consumption has to do with water, remember: 90 percent of the freshwater we use goes to grow the food we eat and manufacture the conveniences we enjoy.

As a consumer, you have a right to say enough is enough. Boycotts, letter campaigns, and press conferences have tremendous power to tell advertisers to stop promoting a "throwaway" lifestyle. And if you think it's only wacky tree huggers waging protests, you might be surprised to know that both the right and the left have used boycotts to great effect.

BONUS TIP: Instead of throwing it away, buy it reusable. Every year, we throw away two billion disposable razors. We could circle the planet end to end with the number of disposable cameras we use and—if you hadn't guessed it by now—the amount of water it takes to produce these items is enormous.

FACT

Many businesses dispose of wastewater into natural freshwater systems. Rivers and lakes can process small quantities of waste. But when these limits are exceeded, water quality declines, and downstream water is no longer usable without expensive treatment.

It takes:
- Seventy-five gallons of water to produce a single ear of corn.
- Six gallons of water to refine a gallon of gasoline.
- Sixty-five gallons of water to manufacture enough steel to make a bicycle.

Between 1940 and 1976, Americans consumed more minerals than did all of humanity up to that point. Each American consumes about eighteen times as much commercially produced energy as a person living in Bangladesh—and about twice as much as our counterparts in Europe and Japan.

Happy Birthday MS. Earth!

For a world that's been pretty good to us, it took an awfully long time—roughly about three hundred thousand years—before civilization realized that maybe we should give our planet its own holiday. We think the first plans for Earth Day started something like this:

CLOUD: Looks like someone is going to be five billion years old tomorrow.

TREE: She sure doesn't look it.

CLOUD: You haven't seen her without her makeup.

TREE: I'm just saying . . .

CLOUD: Did you get her anything?

TREE: What do you get for the planet that has everything?

CLOUD: That's what I mean. If we get her something, she'll expect a gift every year.

TREE:	What if we named a day after her?
CLOUD:	We'd never hear the end of it.
TREE:	You're probably right.

Actually, a senator named Gaylord Nelson believed Earth Day needed to be celebrated every year, with all the pomp and fervor of the most impressive nonsecular holiday. After touring the nation in the mid 1960s, the senator discovered that the environmental issue was nowhere to be found on the nation's political agenda. "People were concerned, but the politicians were not," Nelson said. And so, in a historic press conference in Seattle in September 1969, Nelson announced his plans for a nationwide grassroots demonstration on behalf of the environment to be held April 22, 1970. Everyone was invited to participate. And everyone did. Nearly twenty million demonstrators and thousands of schools and local communities spoke loud and clear—the politicians would make the environment a priority or the voters would find someone who would.

FACT: Twenty-five years after organizing the first Earth Day, Senator Gaylord Nelson was awarded the Presidential Medal of Freedom by President Bill Clinton. The president said of Nelson, "He inspired us to remember that the stewardship of our natural resources is the stewardship of the American Dream."

FACT: Although Earth Day is most often celebrated on April 22, another Earth Day was created by John McConnell, an environmental advocate in San Francisco, on March 21, 1970. But however you choose to celebrate it, we believe Earth Day should be every day.

55

Drops for Crops

The importance of irrigation for agriculture is undeniable, although the amounts of water required for some crops—rice in water-poor areas, for example—may be questionable. According to the Worldwatch Institute, 69 percent of the world's available freshwater is claimed by agriculture. Lacking enough rainwater to replace these vast quantities, more and more regions such as the western United States, India, and northern China rely on overpumping and aquifer depletion to irrigate farms and water livestock.

It takes one thousand tons of water to produce 1 ton of grain. As water becomes scarce and countries are forced to divert irrigation water to cities and industry, they will import more grain. As they do so, water scarcity will be transmitted across national borders via the grain trade. Aquifer depletion is a largely invisible threat, but that does not make it any less real.

—LESTER A. BROWN, Michael Renner, and Brian Halweil, *Vital Signs,* 1999

FACT

In heavily populated cities like Mexico City, Bangkok, and Jakarta, land is sinking as more groundwater is withdrawn to serve the needs of growing populations that can't be replenished by rainfall. In Mexico City, the pumping of groundwater exceeds the natural recharge of the aquifer by as much as 80 percent. Meanwhile, major rivers such as the Nile in Egypt, the Ganges in South Asia, the Yellow River in China, and the Colorado River are dammed and diverted to meet unprecedented demands.

TIP

The future of our blue planet will depend on many innovations, sensible laws, and changes in economic policies. Above all, you can make a difference with a simple change in attitude: instead of looking for ways to meet growing demands for water in your community, become an advocate for more wisely managing what's available.

56

Sharing Scenarios

Given the fact that we live on a round planet, we find a particular truth in the old adage "Everyone lives downstream from someone else." We are entering an age of cooperative survival, where we must recognize the inescapable fact that the water we use belongs to the common good. Yet the potential for conflict remains: Ethiopians have built dams on the upper reaches of the Nile River, reducing the flow into Egypt. In trying to ensure water for its people, the country of Turkey constructed the Southwest Anatolia Project upstream on the Euphrates—striking fears of water depletion into the downstream countries of Syria and Iraq.

Global freshwater supplies are being used up so fast that almost half a billion people already depend on nonrenewable sources, an international conference was told Monday. Water riots such as those in China's Shandong province last month will become more common as people struggle for control of dwindling supplies, said Lester Brown, chairman of the U.S.-based Worldwatch Institute. Thousands of Chinese farmers clashed with police in July after officials cut off water leaking from a dam near Anqiu village in Shandong province, according to a human rights group.

—Reuters News Service, "Global Water Supply Central Issue at Stockholm Conference," reported by CNN.com, August 14, 2000

FACT

OUTLOOK: More countries are recognizing the need for mutual planning and cooperation. The drought-plagued nations of Africa, Namibia, Botswana, and Angola participated in UN-brokered talks to plan for future water needs in the Okavango Basin. India agreed in 1996 to increase flow of the Ganges to its downstream neighbor, Bangladesh, and in 1997 Israel and Jordan signed a water-sharing agreement.

57

Big Blue Battery

Let's face it: Batteries are usually nothing to get excited about. But did you know that in one day the world's tropical seas store the equivalent heat energy of 250 billion barrels of oil? Like a giant battery, these waters hold so much power that scientists believe they may one day provide most of humanity's energy needs. Harnessing this power is called Ocean Thermal Energy Conversion (OTEC)—a concept that has been around since the 1880s. An OTEC test plant is currently in operation in Kailua-Kona, Hawaii.

Proceed Carefully . . .

Like any new technology, OTEC requires caution. The flow of water from a 100-megawatt OTEC plant would equal that of the Colorado River. And that water could be warmer or cooler than when it was originally drawn into the plant. The resulting changes in salinity and temperature could have unforeseen consequences for the local ecology.

Shifting to renewable sources of energy will not be easy. Costs will be higher at first than traditional sources, and ensuring that the new energy is environmentally friendly will take time. This is where you come in: Renewable energy sources like OTEC will never find their way into widespread use if government considers only the immediate bottom line. By supporting government-funded research and testing today, you may be providing a clean energy source for future generations tomorrow.

58

Winds of Climate Change

Is global warming a reality? Are we causing it directly? Or are we simply accelerating a natural cycle? The fact is scientists have not been around long enough to directly measure the entire history and cycle of climate change. However, in September 2003, a study considered to be the most comprehensive ever on climatic history concluded that the earth is warmer now than it has been at any time in the past two thousand years. The study by the United Nations Intergovernmental Panel on Climate Change reconstructed more than a millennia of temperature data, measuring tree growth and conducting extensive studies of ice core samples from Greenland and the Antarctic.

You can't explain this rapid warming of the late twentieth century in any other way. It's a response to a buildup of greenhouse gases in the atmosphere.

—PHILIP JONES, director of the University of East Anglia's climate research unit

Whether you're heating your house or running an errand in your car, you're leaving a carbon dioxide footprint. But here's good news: Changing your footprint is easier than you might think. The EPA estimates that about a third of your carbon dioxide output can be reduced based on your choices of transportation, waste produced, and the type of energy you use at home. Even painting your house and roof lighter colors that reflect light can reduce your need for air conditioning. Calculate the carbon dioxide generated by your fossil fuel use by visiting the American Forests Web site at http://www.americanforests.org/resources/ccc/.

FACT

It is estimated that carbon dioxide emissions account for 83 percent of greenhouse gas. These gases absorb infrared radiation as it is reflected from the surface of the earth, and keep the earth warm. Increasing concentrations of greenhouse gases appear to be causing the earth's temperature to rise as more and more infrared radiation is trapped in the atmosphere. Other greenhouse gases include methane, nitrous oxide, hydrofluorocarbons, perfluorocarbons, and sulphur hexafluoride.

BONUS TIP: Buy products with the Energy Star, an EPA voluntary labeling program that identifies and promotes energy-efficient products. By buying Energy Star–labeled products in 2004, Americans saved enough energy to power twenty-four million homes and avoid the equivalent greenhouse gas emissions from twenty million cars—all the while saving $10 billion. Look for the Energy Star on home electronics, heating and cooling equipment, and appliances. To learn more, visit http://www.energystar.gov.

59

What's in a Name?

You hear the term *global warming* almost every day. But our choice of words may not paint an accurate picture of all the effects caused by rising concentrations of greenhouse gas. This is why many scientists refer to global warming, instead, as *climate change*. The fact is as some regions grow warmer, others are cooling. This change in weather systems could result in floods, droughts, and an increase in violent storms. A 2001 UN Intergovernmental Panel on Climate Change report projected that the earth's average surface temperature will increase between 2.5° and 10.4°F between 1990 and 2100 if no major efforts are undertaken to reduce the emissions of greenhouse gases. Under this scenario, scientists expect a rise in sea level between 3.5 and 34.6 inches, leading to more coastal erosion and flooding during storms.

"From 1995 to 2000 we saw the highest level of North Atlantic hurricane activity ever measured," [Stanley] Goldenberg [a research meteorologist at NOAA's Hurricane Research Division] said. "Compared with the previous twenty-four years there were twice as many hurricanes in the Atlantic, including two and a half times more major hurricanes—those reaching Category 3 strength with winds reaching more than 110 mph—and more than five times as many hurricanes impacting the Caribbean islands.

—"Hurricane Activity Accelerates in U.S. Long-Term Forecast," Environment News Service, July 23, 2001

Even with all the speculation on the causes of climate change, it's a safe bet that the world can't go wrong by reducing carbon emissions. May we suggest a tune-up for your car? A finely tuned car saves up to 9 percent more gasoline than a neglected one. That means if only 100,000 car owners joined the ranks of those who regularly tune their car, we could reduce atmospheric carbon dioxide by 90 million pounds every year.

BONUS TIP: Cut your carbon dioxide footprint an additional five hundred pounds each year by washing your laundry in cold water.

FACT

Scientists have concluded that the destructive power of hurricanes in the North Atlantic and North Pacific has nearly doubled over the past thirty years, at least partly caused by human-induced climate change. This does not necessarily mean that we have contributed to the recent frequency of storms, which most scientists believe is part of a natural cycle. Nevertheless, according to most studies, average temperatures in major hurricane-producing regions have increased by .5° Celsius in the last century. That small increase could make a big difference in hurricane intensity by raising the energy available for storms.

Experts say that global warming is serious, and they are predicting now that by the year 2050, we will be out of party ice.

—DAVID LETTERMAN

A Tip About Aquaculture

Fishermen and growing world populations have begun to complain about slim fishery harvests in the world's oceans. Many once-abundant species have declined from a combination of overfishing, environmental damage, and slow regeneration rates. As a result, aquaculture production—or seafood farming—has increased by more than 300 percent since 1984. This has resulted in greater availability of seafood, but it has created a multifinned Frankenstein. In some cases, aquaculture leads to extensive pollution, decreases immune capacities, and promotes outbreaks of disease among fish. Other types of aquaculture, such as shrimp aquaculture, play a large role in the destruction of coastal habitats, including mangrove swamps, that are needed to make way for shrimp ponds. Ironically, it is these mangroves that act as natural flood barriers and filters and are spawning grounds for many of the wild species that are currently in decline.

We need a global approach to this from all sides. We need to educate people, we need the scientists to create new technologies, we need the engineers to create the networks, we need every human being to be aware of how precious water is and save it. Everybody has to be involved in a very firm and assertive way.

—ISABEL ALLENDE, quoted in Peter Swanson's *Water: The Drop of Life,* 2001

A better understanding of the complexities of fish farming are showing progress in reducing the environmental impacts of aquaculture. By integrating seaweeds, mussels, and other organisms that grow well in waste waters, fish farmers can reduce waste in surrounding waters. In countries such as Chile, some salmon are farmed with a red algae that removes nitrogen and phosphorous wastes from the cages. So before your next all-you-can-eat shrimp buffet bonanza, you might ask how your dinner is farmed *and* caught.

61

Trawling for Dollars

Remember being a kid when your mom would let you lick the bowl of cookie dough? Well, with many popular fish stocks disappearing, today's fishermen are exploring new ways to scrape more food out of the sea. A popular technique—trawling—drags weighted nets along the ocean floor to catch bottom-dwelling fish like shrimp and flounder. The only problem is that these massive trawling nets dredge up thousands of pounds of unwanted fish, known as by-catch, that either die on deck or are discarded, much to the detriment of biodiversity in coastal ecosystems. In some cases, new technologies have allowed trawlers to go deeper than ever—netting fish at depths of up to 2,500 feet, where deep-living species grow. These species tend to regenerate very slowly, so the impacts from trawling can be especially devastating.

Although trawling has been declared illegal in the waters surrounding many countries, it is still very much in use. In fact, trawling may be more widespread than we think. According to the World Resources Institute, only twenty-four countries provided sufficient data in an international survey to map trawling grounds in their waters—leaving speculation that the world's trawling grounds may encompass an area more than twice the size of Brazil.

Trawling has been compared to clear-cutting forests—or wholesale decimation of marine habitats. With habitats wiped out, marine biodiversity plummets, and the fishery that we depend on for food is destroyed. By supporting international treaties banning such shortsighted fishing practices, we can eliminate this threat to the already fraying web of life in our oceans.

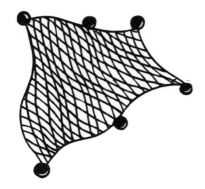

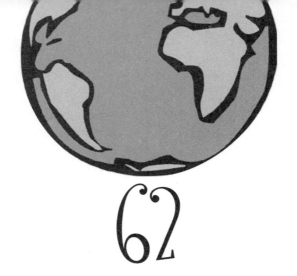

A Dry Look at Toilets

Most people in industrialized nations expect access to indoor toilets. But around the world, the creature comfort that we take for granted is in short supply. In August 2005, experts at the Stockholm Water Week conference proposed an alternative to the traditional water-flushing toilet that would use less water, pollute less, and would be affordable enough for installation in third-world and developing countries. The new "dry" toilets separate urine and excrement, and the materials are recycled into fertilizer. (We're just waiting for one in teal.)

FACT: Basic human needs for water go beyond drinking. Improper disposal of human waste—a practice that leads to a cycle of infection and contamination—remains one of the leading causes of illness and death in the developing world.

FACT: Inadequate water supplies are both a cause and an effect of poverty. Invariably those without adequate and affordable water supplies are the poorest in the society. The effects of inadequate water supply—disease, time and energy expended in daily collection, high unit costs, etc.—exacerbate the poverty trap.

—World Health Organization, 2001
World Water Development Report

FACT

While the average person in the United States flushes away 15,000 liters of water every year, more than 2.6 billion people in the world do not have access to toilets—a shortage that can result in disease, sickness, and death. The United Nations has established a millennium development goal to provide 1.75 billion people with access to their own toilets by 2015. That means ninety-five thousand toilets will have to be installed per day to achieve the goal.

Solutions to future environmental issues often depend on learning new habits. Understanding and advocating new changes and technologies, such as dry toilets, may have global health and economic impacts. (We tip our hat to Sweden, where dry toilets are commonly installed in summer homes.)

Part V

Strange Weather Ahead

Negative Flow

In the southwestern United States, huge increases in thirsty people have sopped up the flow of the Colorado River. Politicians, environmentalists, and industry representatives alike worry that demand for water in the region is unsustainable. Starting in the upper elevations of Wyoming, the river winds through Colorado, Utah, and New Mexico, and the low deserts of the Southwest. But with demands exceeding flow rate, the great river is barely a trickle by the time it reaches its final destination, the Sea of Cortez.

Three hundred twenty-five gallons of water are consumed per person per day in Las Vegas, possibly more than any other city in the world.

—JOSH SEVIN, "Water, Water Everywhere," *Grist Magazine,* December 20, 1999

If surface water can be compared with interest income, and nonrenewable groundwater with capital, then much of the West was living mainly on interest income. California was milking interest and capital in about equal proportion. The plains states, however, were devouring capital as a gang of spendthrift heirs might squander a great capitalist's fortune.

—MARC REISNER, *Cadillac Desert*, 1986

The 1,450-mile Colorado River was known in years past as the American Nile, yet has been so devastated that its waters no longer reach the sea. More than twenty dams, diversion schemes, and a variety of industrial and agricultural pollutants threaten the integrity of this 246,000 square mile watershed from the headwaters in Wyoming, Utah, New Mexico, and Colorado, and through Nevada, Arizona, and California, to the river's desiccated delta at the Gulf of California in northwestern Mexico.

—"Nation's Most Senior River Activist Declares Colorado Most Endangered Watershed," E-Wire Press Release, April 7, 2000

FACT

The Colorado River has supplied an average of 14.6 million acre-feet of water a year over the last century. Demand over the last two decades, however, now exceeds 14.4 million acre-feet a year—and projections indicate it will get worse. According to the federal Bureau of Reclamation, the upper basin states of Wyoming, Colorado, Utah, and New Mexico have plans to increase their take from 4.2 million acre-feet today to 5.4 million in a few decades, bringing annual demand to more than 15 million acre-feet. Adding to the uncertainty are climate predictions for drought that may rob the upper basin of 2 million acre-feet a year.

OUTLOOK: The U.S. Department of the Interior and the seven states with rights to the Colorado have to face the reality of growing water demands in the Southwest. Population booms in Las Vegas and interstate water banking in Arizona are forcing California, which has been using more than its share of water, to come to grips with aggressive water conservation programs. According to the Sierra Club's Regional Conservation Committee's Colorado River Report, "There is significant pressure from the other basin states for California to develop and adhere to a plan that will reduce water consumption in California to 4.4 million acre-feet by 2015. It is, however, not clear that any such plan can be put in place without causing major disruption of California's existing economy. Continued population growth with forecasts of fifty million Californians within thirty years will, if even close to accurate, stress the current system beyond the breaking point."

64

View from the Greenhouse

These days, speculation abounds on climate change. Though we still have many questions, we do know that changes in climate have resulted in temperature extremes, flooding, and drought around the world. Because of the complexity of hydrological cycles, scientists are still struggling to make precise predictions about the future of climate change. But most scientists now believe precipitation will probably increase in some areas and decrease in others; changes in water levels and temperatures could affect the survival and growth of organisms, such as coral reefs; and rising seas could invade coastal freshwater supplies.

Portage is "a glacier that's almost out of water; it's thinned dramatically," said U.S. Geological Survey geologist Bruce Molnia, the author of the book *Glaciers of Alaska*. About 98 percent of Alaska's glaciers are retreating or stagnant, he said. Alaskan glaciers add 13.2 trillion gallons of melted water to the seas each year—the equivalent of more than 13 million Olympic-sized swimming pools, University of Alaska in Fairbanks scientists concluded after a decade of studying glaciers with airborne lasers. The rate of glacier runoff has doubled over just a few decades, they found. Alaska's melting glaciers are the number-one reason the oceans are rising, Molnia said.

—SETH BORENSTEIN, "The Melting Tip of the Iceberg," *St. Paul Pioneer Press*, August 3, 2003

With so many factors playing a role in environmental change, improved global literacy and education is paramount. In its simplest form, literacy involves general awareness, knowledge, and understanding of the human environment and its associated problems; the skills to deal with such problems; and the need to preserve the environment as the resource base for meeting human needs.

FACT

In addition to the introduction of greenhouse gases into the atmosphere, scientists must wrestle with ever-changing factors, such as deforestation, urbanization, and the overuse of water supplies, that affect the hydrological cycle, making predictions even harder.

BONUS TIP: Join the global march—from your desk chair. Join forces with the National Resources Defense Council, the Sierra Club, the Surfrider Foundation, the Rainforest Alliance, the Union of Concerned Scientists, and other concerned organizations in this virtual march against global warming. Begin marching at http://www.stopglobal-warming.org.

BONUS TIP: Get a report card from your utility company. Many utility companies provide home energy audits to help consumers identify areas in their homes that may not be energy efficient. In addition, many utility companies offer rebate programs to help pay for the cost of energy-efficient upgrades.

Desert by Numbers

Humans have unprecedented abilities to shape the earth. We can harness the power of mighty rivers and literally move mountains. There are, however, unintentional effects of our progress. One of these is desertification—the combination of natural climate changes and human activities that are literally turning arid and semiarid areas of Africa, Asia, Latin America, the Caribbean, and the northern Mediterranean into deserts. Clearing away plants to make room for farms can actually jeopardize a local water supply.

I find man utterly unaware of what his wealth is or his fundamental capability is. He says time and again, "We can't afford it." For instance, we are saying now that we can't afford to do anything about pollution but after the costs of not doing something about pollution have multiplied many fold beyond what it would cost to correct it now, we will spend many fold what it would cost us now to correct it.

—BUCKMINSTER FULLER (1895-1983), *The World Game,* 1969

TIP

Locally, you can support international "Plant a Tree" efforts to slow the march of deserts, absorb excess carbon dioxide, and improve the quality of life around the world. Some trees, such as acacia albida, even do double duty as nitrogen-fixing plants that provide naturally poor soil with much-needed nutrients.

BONUS TIP: Invest in rainforest communities. The Protect-an-Acre Program is an alternative to "buy-an-acre" programs, which tend to ignore the fact that there are often people who depend on the forest and have lived in the forest sustainably for centuries. Protect-an-Acre provides funding to help forest peoples gain legal recognition of their territories, develop locally based alternative economic initiatives, and resist destructive practices such as logging and fossil fuel development. For information about how you can support the Protect-an-Acre program, visit the Rainforest Action Network Web site at http://www.ran.org.

FACT

Plants act as nature's sponges. They soak up water and slowly release it throughout the year. This provides reliable river flows, replenishes groundwater, and releases moisture back into the atmosphere. Remove the plants and croplands erode, floods become more frequent, groundwater reserves disappear and the climate changes.

Scientists now believe that much of Tanzania—home to Mount Kilimanjaro and Lake Victoria—is rapidly turning into desert, due to drought and deforestation. More than 998,000 acres of forests are razed in Tanzania every year. At that rate, researchers believe that desert sands will claim half the country by the year 2050.

OUTLOOK: Growing desertification affects every aspect of life in regions throughout the world, from water availability to food production. African nations have recognized this threat and have agreed to combat desertification at national, subregional, and regional levels by enacting laws requiring environmental protection and sustainable development.

Making a Stink About Methane

Your parents warned you about getting enough green vegetables. What did they know, anyway? A lot, apparently. Now, it turns out that eating more vegetables and less meat may have a significant impact on global warming. According to a report by the environmental group EarthSave International, the most significant source of climate change over the next half century may very well be animal agriculture—not cars and power plants that emit carbon dioxide from burning fossil fuels.

There is some evidence that average wave heights are slowly rising, and that freak waves of eighty or ninety feet are becoming more common. Wave heights off the coast of England have risen an average of 25 percent over the past couple of decades, which converts to a twenty-foot increase in the highest waves over the next half century. One cause may be the tightening of environmental laws, which has reduced the amount of oil flushed into the oceans by oil tankers. Oil spreads across water in a film several molecules thick and inhibits the generation of capillary waves, which in turn prevent the wind from getting a "grip" on the sea. Plankton releases a chemical that has the same effect, and plankton levels in the North Atlantic have dropped dramatically. Another explanation is that the recent warming trend—some call it the greenhouse effect—has made storms more frequent and severe. Waves have destroyed docks and buildings in Newfoundland, for example, that haven't been damaged for decades.

—SEBASTIAN JUNGER, *The Perfect Storm*, 1998

FACT

Animal agriculture produces more than one hundred million tons of methane a year—about 85 percent from livestock digestion and 15 percent from manure lagoons used to store untreated feces. Methane is twenty-one times more powerful a greenhouse gas than carbon dioxide.

TIP

EarthSave says reducing methane can have a cooling effect on the planet in short order because methane cycles out of the atmosphere in eight years, as compared to carbon dioxide, which stays in the atmosphere for decades. And that reduction may be as simple as adding a little more roughage to your diet.

BONUS TIP: Rainforest beef is typically found in fast food hamburgers or processed beef products. In both 1993 and 1994 the United States imported over two hundred million pounds of fresh and frozen beef from Central American countries. Two-thirds of these countries' rainforests have been cleared, in part to raise cattle whose meat is exported to profit the U.S. food industry. When it enters the United States, the beef is not labeled with its country of origin, so there is no way to trace it to its source. Reducing your consumption of beef will reduce demand for it, cutting back on pressure to clear more forests for cattle. For more information on the connection between beef and the environment, contact Earthsave International, 1509 Seabright Avenue, Suite B1, Santa Cruz, CA 95062; 1-800-362-3648; http://www.earthsave.org.

Carbon dioxide is largely produced by the burning of fossil fuels, especially coal, and especially our use of inefficient vehicles for transportation. But not often mentioned is the fossil fuel used to raise farm animals. A factory cow is a fossil fuel machine, not a solar-powered ruminant whose wastes fertilize the fields to produce more grass for the cow to eat. When you eat beans, for example, you use $1/27$ the amount of fossil fuel to produce a calorie of energy as you do when you eat beef. You get the same food energy producing only four percent of the carbon dioxide that a person eating beef does. Another fact we don't talk about: cattle produce almost one fifth of global methane emissions. Cattle fart. Big time. Their gas is methane. Methane is actually twenty-four times as potent as carbon dioxide in causing climate chaos.

—STEVE BOYAN, Ph. D.,
"How our Food Choices Can Help Save the Environment," http://www.earthsave.org

Express Yourself

She was named one of the twentieth century's most influential people by *Time* magazine. Yet, Rachel Carson hardly looked like an activist. Shy as a young girl, she had an unbridled love for birds and nature and turned her interests to a degree in zoology, teaching, and ultimately writing. Combining her literary passion with her love of nature, she published her first book, *Under the Sea-Wind*. This was followed by *The Sea Around Us*, a national best-seller that explored the origins and geology of the sea. But her greatest influence sprang from her research into the abuse of chemical pesticides. As she learned more about the effects of DDT, parathion, and malathion on local ecosystems and habitats, Carson realized that the natural world that she loved was under threat. Her 1962 book, *Silent Spring*, talked openly about the dangers of pesticides and herbicides and is widely considered the start of the modern environmentalist movement.

At the release of *Silent Spring,* Rachel Carson was threatened with lawsuits, labeled "hysterical," vilified by the chemical industry, and unsupported by the media. Yet she remained confident in her findings. With intelligence, dedication, and a respect for the living world, she questioned the way things were—and asked if they could not be made better.

TIP

The price of clean water, clean skies, and a healthy natural world is constant vigilance. Like Rachel Carson, understanding environmental issues, community outreach, and the courage to express your views can make a difference for generations to come.

The book showed the presence of toxic chemicals in water and on land as long-lasting and a threat to many creatures. It raised concern among the public, including President John F. Kennedy, who formed a committee to investigate the effects of DDT. Carson died on April 14, 1964, before the results of the research were announced, but because of her work, the Environmental Protection Agency was established as a Cabinet-level position, and, in 1972, the use of DDT was made illegal.

Holding Back a Flood

Hurricanes are unprecedented displays of the force of nature, with sustained winds that can reach two hunderd miles per hour and storm surges that devastate communities. These ferocious superstorms gather strength from thermal energy stored in tropical and subtropical waters and are so powerful that 1 percent of their energy, if harnessed, could meet all the power, fuel, and heating requirements of the United States for an entire year. Yet, for all their power, hurricanes lose force when they come in contact with wetlands—which can buffer coastal cities against storms and rising sea levels.

FACT

For every 2.7 miles of wetlands, storm surges are reduced by about one foot. During the South Asian tsunami of December 2004, mangrove forests growing along the coastlines helped reduce the impact of the surging tsunami by absorbing some of the energy of the waves.

The cost of replacing the natural flood-control function of five thousand acres of drained wetlands in Minnesota was found to be $1.5 million annually. On the other hand, structural answers to flooding—dams and levees—can cost hundreds of millions of dollars. Now, if that were your money . . .

TIP

Human health is tied directly to wetlands health. Experts believe the preservation of wetlands may ultimately provide a better—and, in some cases, cheaper—answer to polluted waters, floods, depleted groundwater aquifers, declining water quality, and exposed shorelines than expensive high-tech solutions. Remember that the next time a coastal golf course or housing project is proposed in your neighborhood.

BONUS TIP: Nearly three-quarters of America's remaining wetlands are on private lands. Support government-subsidized easement and set-aside programs to help farmers keep their wetlands environmentally friendly. There are organizations, like Ducks Unlimited, that help farmers enroll in these programs and distribute planting equipment to help them replant natural grasses on lands no longer used for agriculture.

A Crystal Clear Revolution

Two decades ago, as an idealistic young man intent on helping India's rural poor, Rajendra Singh traveled to northwestern Rajasthan, which was suffering water shortages from excessive groundwater extraction. Shortly after he arrived in the impoverished Alwar district, two things became clear to Singh. The first was that managing water wisely was the key to helping drought-prone villages in the region. The second was that farmers were pumping far too much groundwater.

"If you replenish water, that is a green revolution," Singh told me. "But if you destroy your water capital, what kind of green revolution is that?"

An old villager showed Singh the numerous earthen dams in the district that had fallen into disrepair, their reservoirs filled with silt. They were remnants of a rainwater collection tradition that dated back five thousand years in India, a system that used the natural terrain to channel and store the brief monsoon downpours for year-round use.

But community rainwater collection schemes fell out of favor during British rule and after independence in 1947; their neglect, coupled with overpumping of groundwater, led to a crisis in villages throughout western India. Singh became consumed with the idea of building *johads*, gradually helping villagers erect the earthen and stone structures all over Rajasthan.

Today he is perhaps the best known of a large group of people who have revived India's ancient rainwater harvesting techniques, which use not only dams but also underground storage tanks and large concrete-lined reservoirs. Singh's organization—financed by the Ford Foundation, among others—has forty-five full-time employees and 230 part-time workers. He spends eight months a year on the road, rarely seeing his wife and son and often sleeping in the backseat of his chauffeur-driven car at night, no small hardship given India's chaotic, treacherous, and polluted highways.

—FEN MONTAIGNE, "Water Pressure," *National Geographic Magazine,* September 2002

Afterword

In writing *Hold Your Water!* we looked at the state of our planet's water in much the same way a kid in auto shop pulls apart a carburetor: peering into the function of our oceans, lakes, rivers, and streams, and examining some of the things each of us does that affect the health of those habitats. Everything looked okay on the surface, but clearly there were rumblings. Activists and politicians were butting heads. There was either too much legislation or too little. Some people pointed fingers, while others said, "It will all sort itself out."

So who was right?

All we knew was we loved water and, quite frankly, we were fans of the coral reefs and salmon runs and surging rivers that inspired writers, poets, artists, retirees, goof-offs, and honeymooners since the first love-struck pioneer paddled his sweetheart across the Poconos. We weren't going to let our world's most magical element go without a fight—or at least a good argument. With plentiful resources and small populations, this blue planet of ours has been able to sustain and support us for a long time. But, as you've seen throughout the various pages of this book, the supplies are no longer guaranteed. We have challenges ahead of us, and we may have to deal with some unpleasant facts. But the sooner we understand the impacts of our environmental policies, and our own environmental actions, the sooner we can address them.

In many ways we already have. In the short span between the 1950s and 1970s, the National Air Pollution Control Act, the Clean Air Act, the Clean Water Act, and the National Environmental Policy Act were passed in the United States. We've phased out many chemical contaminants that once infiltrated our groundwater. Industrialized nations are recognizing the economic value of wind power, solar energy, drip irrigation technology, and alternative fuels. More people are realizing that many of our subsidized resources may, in fact, be encouraging waste, particularly water waste, leading to much more expensive problems down the road.

We've learned the incalculable value of wetlands. Not just for their beauty, but for the fundamental economic benefits they provide in flood control, water filtration, and wildlife diversity and protection. We've learned that water knows no political boundaries, and that in the end, another country's problems are our problems. We've learned that everything we do, everything we eat, and everything we make has some relationship to the world of water around us.

Now, more than ever, we must value nature's services, with an eye toward sustainability. Of course, we can always do better. With the latest knowledge, we can finally put some of our old bad habits aside. And, what the heck, we can—and should—openly speak our mind. We owe that much to our planet. So if someone you know drops a cigarette butt out a window, hit them with the facts. If your local school district starts cutting science programs—the first step toward giving young people the tools they need to solve tomorrow's problems—write a letter so impassioned, you can hear the symphonic strings. If you think fossil fuels are contributing to global warming, buy a hybrid car or ride your bike to work. Even if you're sixty-five years old, and you just truly noticed your first flower, tell someone. Without a hint of embarrassment, let them know how utterly amazing nature is. Sometimes the best activism is simply spreading the word that our planet, our water, and all the inhabitants that rely on it are worth protecting. And if you still need a tip, try this: Wake your husband or wife or kids up early one Sunday morning. Smile politely as they yell, complain, and stomp their feet at the intrusion. Say very little, except that you want to show them something. Take them to the beach, or a lake, or a wetland. Or sit on a rock beside a stream, watch—and listen.

Appendixes

Quick Tips for Water Conservation in the Home

In the kitchen
- Use an aerator and/or a water flow–reducer attachment on your tap to reduce your water usage.
- Always turn taps off tightly so they do not drip.
- Promptly repair any leaks in and around your taps. (One leak can waste several thousand liters of water per year.)
- When hand-washing dishes, never run water continuously. Wash dishes in a partially filled sink and then rinse them using the spray attachment on your tap.
- If you have an electric dishwasher, use it only to wash full loads, and use the shortest cycle possible. Many dishwashers have a conserver/water-miser cycle.
- When cleaning fruit and vegetables, never do so under a continuously running tap. Wash them in a partially filled sink and then rinse them quickly under the tap.

In the bathroom
About 65 percent of indoor home water use occurs in our bathrooms, and toilets are the single greatest water users.
- When washing or shaving, partially fill the sink and use that water rather than running the tap continuously. (This saves about 60 percent of the water normally used.) Use short bursts of water to clean razors.
- When brushing your teeth, turn the water off while you are actually brushing instead of running it continuously. Then use the tap again for rinsing and use short bursts of water for cleaning your brush. (This saves about 80 percent of the water normally used.)

- Always turn taps off tightly so they do not drip.
- Promptly repair any leaks in and around taps.
- Use aerators and/or water flow-reducer devices on all your taps.
- Use either low-flow showerheads or adjustable flow-reducer devices on your showerheads. (They reduce flow by at least 25 percent.)

In the laundry room
- Wash only full loads in your washing machine.
- Use the shortest cycle possible for washing clothes, and use the "suds-saver" feature if your machine has one.
- If your washer has an adjustable water-level indicator, set the dial to use only as much water as is really necessary.
- If you have a septic system, spread out your washing to avoid heavy-use days that could overload the system.

In the yard and garden
- Grass that is green does not need water. Water is required when the grass starts to develop a black tinge along the top. Recovery is almost immediate when water is applied at this stage. Blackening does not hurt grass; browning does.
- Do not overwater in anticipation of a shortage. Soil cannot store extra water.
- Use shut-off timers or on-off timers, if possible. Do not turn on sprinklers and leave for the day.
- Water during the cool part of the day, in the morning or evening. Do not water on windy days.

In the outdoors
- Do not wash in the lake or river.
- Wash your dishes away from the water's edge, moving into the bush approximately thirty-five feet. Use sand instead of soap to scrub them clean.
- Do not dump waste food or garbage in the water.
- Clean fish well away from the water's edge.
- Build latrines well back from the water's edge.
- Pack out all nondegradable waste, such as cans, bottles, tinfoil, and plastic.
- Fill outboard motors over land, not over water.

Source: Engagement and Outreach Sustainable Water Use Branch, Environment Canada

Quick Tips for Smart Seafood Dining

Best Choices

- Albacore/Tombo tuna (Pacific)
- Calamari/squid (Pacific)
- Catfish (farmed)
- Caviar (farmed, sturgeon)
- Clams (farmed)
- Dungeness crab
- Halibut (Alaska)
- Mahimahi/dolphinfish/dorado
- Mussels (farmed)
- New Zealand cod/Hoki
- Oysters (farmed)
- Rainbow trout (farmed)
- Salmon (California/Alaska wild-caught—most salmon is farmed. See avoid list.)
- Striped bass (farmed)
- Sturgeon (farmed)
- Tilapia (farmed)

Avoid

- Bluefin tuna
- Caviar (Beluga, Caspian sturgeon)
- Chilean seabass/Patagonia tooth fish
- Cod (Atlantic)
- Lingcod
- Monkfish
- Orange roughy
- Rockfish/Pacific red snapper/rock cod
- Sablefish/butterfish/black cod
- Salmon (farmed)
- Sea scallops (Atlantic)
- Shark (all)
- Shrimp/prawns (wild-caught, international, or farmed)
- Spot prawns (trawl-caught)
- Swordfish

For the complete list, see the Web site of the Monterey Bay Aquarium's Seafood Watch Program, http://www.seafoodwatch.org.

APPENDIX 3
Pathogens–When Good Water Goes Bad

Microorganisms
SOURCE: Sewage discharges and farm runoff can introduce E coli bacteria, cryptosporidium, and other harmful microorganisms.
PROBLEMS: Gastrointestinal illness, severe in people with weak immune systems.
HOT SPOTS: New Haven, Michigan; San Antonio, Texas; any place with treatment or pipe system breakdowns.

Arsenic
SOURCE: Occurs naturally in groundwater and sometimes as a residue of mining and other industrial operations.
PROBLEMS: A strong poison at high doses; at low doses linked to cancer, diabetes, and other diseases.
HOT SPOTS: Albuquerque, New Mexico; Norman, Oklahoma; towns throughout the Southwest.

MTBE
SOURCE: A fuel additive designed to reduce air pollution that has turned into a swift, efficient groundwater polluter through spills and storage tank leaks.
PROBLEMS: Stomach, liver, and nervous system effects, possible cancer risk.
HOT SPOTS: Pascoag, Rhode Island; Santa Monica, California; New Hampshire.

Perchlorate
SOURCE: A component of solid rocket fuel, munitions, and fireworks; has leaked from at least fifty-eight U.S. military bases and manufacturing plants.
PROBLEMS: Interferes with functioning of the thyroid gland.
HOT SPOTS: Riverside, California; Bourne, Massachusetts; contamination confirmed in twenty states.

THMs
SOURCE: Trihalomethanes form when chlorine reacts with organic material, from decayed leaves to feces, in water; extremely common contaminant.
PROBLEMS: Linked to bladder cancer, with some evidence of miscarriage risk.
HOT SPOTS: Waco, Texas, and the Washington, D.C., suburbs.

APPENDIX 4

A Look at Your Water Bill

Is water a basic human right or is it a need? The distinction may be crucial over the next twenty years as companies push to provide this resource on a for-profit basis. As a "human right," governments would work to ensure that all people have equal access to water on a nonprofit basis. A privatized system may have some short-term advantages to local governments, but the addition of profit margins may ultimately be reflected in higher water bills and loss of access to the poorest users.

The following sampling of quarterly water bills demonstrates the costs American consumers pay to private companies for drinkable water:

Costs of Private U.S. Water Systems Quarterly Bill
(Based on U.S Average of Approximately $.50-.55 per cubic meter)
Peoria, Illinois $100.17
Bloomsburg, Pennsylvania $94.69
Hoboken, New Jersey $88.50
Camden, New Jersey $74.42
Atlanta, Georgia $51.00
Jersey City, New Jersey $49.80
Leominster, Massachusetts $44.70
Covina, California $35.80
U.S. average (public and private) $47.50

Costs of Water—Industrialized Nations
Compared to other countries, Americans are getting quite a deal—on the average. Even with the privatization of water systems, water rates in the United States are low compared to those of other developed countries.

Country	Cost Per Cubic Meter (U.S. Dollars)
Germany	$1.91
Denmark	$1.64
Belgium	$1.54
Netherlands	$1.25
France	$1.23
United Kingdom of Great Britain and Northern Ireland	$1.18
Italy	$0.76

Country	Cost Per Cubic Meter (U.S. Dollars)
Finland	$0.69
Ireland	$0.63
Sweden	$0.58
Spain	$0.57
USA	$0.51
Australia	$0.50
South Africa	$0.47
Canada	$0.40

Costs of Water—Developing Nations

In developing countries where water supplies are deficient, the poor are forced to pay even higher rates. Those without a house connection are often forced to obtain water from informal street vendors at up to one hundred times the cost. If a household without running water in Vientiane, Lao, were to use as much water as the average American home, they would spend approximately $1,250 on water every quarter.

City	Cost of water for domestic use (house connection: 10 m³/month) in US$/m³	Price charged by informal vendors vendors in US $/m³
Vientiane (Lao PDR)	0.11	14.68
Mandalay (Myanmar)	0.81	11.33
Faisalabad (Pakistan)	0.11	7.38
Bandung (Indonesia)	0.12	6.05
Manila (Philippines)	0.11	4.74
Cebu (Philippines)	0.33	4.17
Phnom Penh (Cambodia)	0.09	1.64
Ulaanbaatar (Mongolia)	0.04	1.51
Hanoi (Vietnam)	0.11	1.44
Ho Chi Minh City (Vietnam)	0.12	1.08
Karachi (Pakistan)	0.14	0.81
Dhaka (Bangladesh)	0.08	0.42
Jakarta (Indonesia)	0.16	0.31

APPENDIX 5

Solving the Water Crisis?

Solutions to future water problems won't be easy. But groups like Water Policy International believe the following strategies could ensure the health of today's aquatic ecosystems and provide enough water for flourishing communities:

1. **Decision-making frameworks or processes** that recognize aquatic ecosystems and the critical role they play, and that allow aquatic ecosystem functions to be identified and valued in the same context as off-stream or direct water uses by people. These frameworks are primarily law- or policy-based.

2. **Appropriate scientific and technical tools** for quantitatively determining the appropriate water allocations for maintenance of desired aquatic ecosystem functions.

3. **Appropriate management tools and measures** that can be used to manage people's demands and impacts on water resources so that water remains or is made available for aquatic ecosystems.

4. A comprehensive **strategy for implementation** of the management measures that will support water allocations for aquatic ecosystems.

Source: Heather MacKay © 2000/1 Water Policy International Ltd.

APPENDIX 6

Sample Advocacy Letters

Sample Advocacy Letter to a Government Representative

Your name
Your address
Date

Senator _____
U.S. Senate
Washington, D.C. 20510

Dear Senator _____

OR

Rep. _____
U.S. House of Representatives
Washington, D.C. 20515

Dear Senator (or Representative) _____,

I write to seek your support for:

TIP 1: FILL IN THE ISSUE YOU ARE WRITING ABOUT. FOR EXAMPLE:
. . . the U.S. Environmental Protection Agency's long-standing and highly successful environmental education initiative.

TIP 2: STATE THE PROBLEM:
Although money has been appropriated by Congress for environmental education at the EPA, the EPA has indicated it may not allocate the funds for this program.

TIP 3: IDENTIFY THE ACTION YOU WANT YOUR REPRESENTATIVE TO TAKE:
I urge you to communicate to EPA that Congress expects the agency to follow its mandate for funding this program in the next fiscal year and that EPA should recommend sufficient funding for the program in the future.

TIP 4: MAKE A STRONG APPEAL FOR YOUR CASE, CITING BACKGROUND, DATES, STUDIES, ETC:
Environmental education creates an informed citizenry that has the knowledge and skills to understand complex environmental issues and make responsible decisions. By supporting environmental education, we are ensuring that our country will be able to sustainably manage our valuable natural resources and compete in a global economy.

Environmental education is strongly supported by the public. Eliminating or underfunding EPA's environmental education program would be a major setback to our nation's environmental literacy. In response to Congress's mandate for a strong, interdisciplinary environmental education program housed at EPA, the agency has built a highly effective and popular interdisciplinary program that teaches millions of young people, educators, business people, and the public how to understand and grapple with environmental challenges.

TIP 5: SUMMARIZE AND RESTATE YOUR REASON FOR WRITING:

I appreciate Congress's past support and oversight of funds allocated for environmental education at EPA. Please do all you can to guarantee that this federal environmental education effort remains strong.

Sincerely,
(Your Name)

Source: New Century Learning Unit 2, "The Natural World,"
George Mason University—New Century College, excerpt from course curriculum 2003

Sample letter to the editor of a newspaper opinion section

Your name
Your address
Date

Dear Editor,

Since the passage of the Clean Water Act in 1972 huge strides have been made in cleaning up our nation's waters. As we've tackled the obvious eyesores, less obvious clean water problems have been on the rise. Last Monday (NAME OF LOCAL REPRESENTATIVE) had the opportunity to put our community on the path to cleaner water and a more healthy and sustainable environment and economy. In countless polls voters say clean water is a top concern. However, instead of choosing to move us forward on the path to clean water, (NAME OF LOCAL REPRESENTATIVE) has decided to leave us treading water.

In a recent vote on (NAME OF BILL), (NAME OF LOCAL REPRESENTATIVE) ignored the concerns of the American people and chose to instead decrease our understanding of water quality problems, seriously undermine environmental enforcement efforts, and hamper clean water progress. He/She is proposing to weaken environmental enforcement by proposing to cut programs that provide critical monies and technical expertise to local agencies charged with keeping their waters clean. He/She is even proposing to side-step the will of the people to develop voluntary programs to replace mandated requirements that will make local water bodies cleaner and safer. I call on Representatives [INSERT NAMES OF YOUR REPS HERE] and Senators [INSERT NAMES OF SENATORS HERE] to restore these cuts to our vital clean water programs.

Sincerely,
Your name

APPENDIX 7

Getting to Know the Clean Water Act

The Clean Water Act was the first comprehensive national clean water legislation to address growing public concerns for water pollution. Enacted in 1972, it sets a national goal to restore and protect the biological, chemical, and physical integrity of the nation's waters. Meeting that goal involves maintaining water quality that protects balanced indigenous populations of fish, shellfish, and wildlife and preserves recreational use of those waters. States, territories, and authorized tribes have major responsibilities under the Clean Water Act, including assessing the quality of their waters. That information is compiled by the EPA and sent to Congress every two years in the National Water Quality Inventory. Using this information, experts can learn if our waters are meeting standards for drinking, for use by aquatic life, for fish and shellfish consumption, as well as recreational, agricultural, industrial, and domestic uses. The NWQI gives an idea of the condition of the nation's waters. But, because many states only test problem areas and often have different sampling techniques and standards, it does not give the entire picture.

Key points of the Clean Water Act include:
1. Requirements for major industries to meet performance standards to ensure pollution control.
2. Requirements for states and tribes to set specific water quality criteria and develop pollution control programs appropriate to their waters.
3. Funding for states and communities to meet local clean water infrastructure needs.
4. Protection for valuable wetlands and other aquatic habitats through a permitting process that ensures environmentally sound use.

Fifty Environmental Organizations Worth Supporting

American Rivers
American Zoo and Aquarium
  Association
Center for a Livable Future
Clean Water Fund
Clean Water Network
Conservation International
Center for Renewable Energy and
  Sustainable Technology (CREST)
Defenders of Wildlife
Ducks Unlimited
Earth First
Earth Justice Defense Fund
EarthSave International
EarthWatch
Energy and Environmental Research
  Center
Environmental Defense
Environmental Literacy Council
Friends of the Earth
Global Recourse Action Center for the
  Environment (GRACE)
Greenpeace International
Keep America Beautiful
Kids for a Clean Environment (Kids
  FACE)
League of Conservation Voters
National Audubon Society
National Coalition for Marine
  Conservation

National Environmental Trust
National Parks Conservation
  Association
National Wildlife Federation
National Resources Defense Council
The Nature Conservancy
The Ocean Conservancy
The Ocean Project
Oceana
Project Aware Foundation
Public Interest Research Group
Quiksilver Foundation
Rainforest Alliance
Restore America's Estuaries
Seas the Day
Scripps Institute of Oceanography
Sierra Club
Surfrider Foundation
United Nations Environment Fund
Waterkeeper Alliance
Wetlands International
The Wilderness Society
Woods Hole Research Center
World Resources Institute
World Wildlife Fund (WWF)
Worldwatch Institute
Last, but certainly not least, the
  Wyland Foundation

APPENDIX 9

Start Now

WATER BY THE NUMBERS

I pledge to . . .	Amount of Water Saved per Year
☐ Place a sealed plastic bottle in my toilet tank.	1,369 gallons
☐ Fix a faucet that drips.	5,460 gallons
☐ Install a low-flow showerhead.	26,000 gallons
☐ Flush the toilet one less time per day.	1,825 gallons
☐ Switch to an air-assisted toilet.	38,428 gallons
☐ Take showers instead of baths.	6,205 gallons
☐ Reduce my shower time by five minutes.	9,125 gallons
☐ Turn off the sink while brushing my teeth.	3,650 gallons
☐ Cut the amount of meat I eat in half.	250,000 gallons
☐ Run my dishwasher only when it is full.	4,800 gallons
☐ Check all washing machine hose connections for leaks.	6,000 gallons
☐ Wash clothes only when I have a full load.	7,200 gallons
☐ Turn the water off while I shampoo and condition my hair.	2,600 gallons
☐ Upgrade to a high-efficiency washing machine.	5,000 gallons
☐ Turn off the water while I shave.	5,200 gallons
☐ Avoid using my toilet as a wastebasket.	6,000 gallons
☐ Capture tap water while I wait for hot water to come down the pipes. Catch the flow in a watering can to use later on houseplants or my garden.	3,600 gallons
☐ Rinse dishes in a sink half full of water rather than running the faucet.	4,200 gallons
☐ Use the least amount of detergent possible when washing dishes.	1,800 gallons
☐ Keep a bottle of drinking water in the refrigerator instead of running cool tap water.	3,600 gallons
☐ Avoid defrosting frozen foods with running water.	1,800 gallons
☐ Clean vegetables in a bucket or water-filled sink, not with running water.	3,000 gallons
☐ Use the garbage disposal less.	1,800 gallons
☐ Install inline water heaters or recalculating systems.	10,950 gallons
☐ Avoid prerinsing dishes before loading the dishwasher. (Tests show that prerinsing doesn't impove cleaning; it just wastes water.)	6,500 gallons
☐ Close the drain before turning on the water when taking a bath.	1,095 gallons

☐ Fill my bathtub only halfway.	1,825 gallons
☐ Recycle just one aluminum can a day.	210 gallons
☐ Turn off the faucet while washing my hands.	1,825 gallons
☐ Take Navy showers—get wet, turn off the water, soap, scrub, then turn on the water to rinse.	13,140 gallons
☐ Xeriscape–replace my lawn and high-water-using trees and plants with less thirsty ones.	18,000 gallons
☐ Water my lawn in the early morning instead of mid-day.	84,240 gallons
☐ Dispose of hazardous materials and oil properly.	250,000 gallons
☐ Use a broom instead of a hose to clean my driveway and sidewalks.	7,200 gallons
☐ Cover my swimming pool.	10,800 gallons
☐ Adjust my sprinklers so that water lands on my lawn or garden, not the sidewalk.	6,000 gallons
☐ Put a layer of mulch around trees and plants.	15,000 gallons
☐ Avoid watering the lawn on a windy day.	300 gallons
☐ Limit the amount of water used to water my lawn on cool and overcast days.	9,000 gallons
☐ Avoid watering my lawn on rainy days.	15,000 gallons
☐ Set lawn mower blades one notch higher.	1,800 gallons
☐ Tell my children not to play with the garden hose.	150 gallons
☐ Adjust my irrigation system seasonally.	50,000 gallons
☐ Manage pool water to avoid draining and refilling.	20,000 gallons
☐ Deep soak my garden once weekly rather than sprinkle lightly several times a week in the summer.	650 gallons
☐ Take my car to a commercial car wash instead of washing it at home.	384 gallons
☐ Choose a car wash that recycles water.	6,600 gallons
☐ Use a bucket (not a running hose) while washing my car at home.	7,200 gallons
☐ Choose a car that gets ten miles per gallon above average (average car is rated 22 mpg).	4,621 gallons
☐ Slow down and drive at 50 mph instead of 70 mph.	1,080 gallons

Total Water Saved _____ gallons

FACT: If you followed every tip, you'd save enough water to fill over fifty swimming pools.

Glossary

Acid rain. Rain that has become more acidic from falling through air pollutants, primarily sulfur dioxide, and dissolving them.

Algae. One-celled or many-celled plants that carry out photosynthesis in streams, lakes, oceans, and other waters. Algae forms the base of the food chain.

Algae blooms. Rapid growth of algae on the surface of lakes, streams, or ponds; stimulated by nutrient enrichment.

Alkali. Any strongly basic substance of hydroxide and carbonate, such as soda, potash, etc., that is soluble in water and increases the pH of a solution.

Aquaculture. Growing and harvesting of fish and shellfish in land-based ponds.

Aquifer. Natural underground area of earth, gravel, or porous stone that contains groundwater.

Bacteria. Single-celled organisms, invisible to the naked eye.

Bioaccumulation (bioconcentration). A term used to describe a process that occurs when levels of toxic substances increase in an organism over time, due to continued exposure.

Biodegradable. Capable of being broken down by living organisms into inorganic compounds.

Biodegrade. When microorganisms break down items into simple substances and use this process for food.

Biological diversity (biodiversity). The variety of different species, the genetic variability of each species, and the variety of different ecosystems that they form.

Biomagnification (biological magnification). A cumulative increase in the concentrations of a persistent substance in successively higher levels of the food chain.

Coliform bacteria. A group of organisms usually found in the colons of animals and humans. The presence of coliform bacteria in water is an indicator of possible pollution by fecal material.

Delta. An alluvial deposit made of rock particles (sediment and debris) dropped by a stream as it enters a body of water.

Depletion. Loss of water from surface water reservoirs or groundwater aquifers at a rate greater than that of recharge.

Desertification. The degradation of terrestrial ecosystems as a result of deforestation, overgrazing, poor soil, and irrigation management.

Diazinon. Chemical found in some pesticides that was originally developed during World War II from nerve gas.

Drinking water standards. Standards established by state agencies, the U.S. Public Health Service, and the EPA for the quality of water used for drinking in the United States.

El Niño. Recurrent fluctuation in the atmospheric pressures and surface water temperature in the tropical Pacific.

Environmental Protection Agency (EPA). Government agency founded by President Richard Nixon in 1970 to establish and enforce environmental standards for the United States.

Estuary. A place where saltwater and freshwater mix, usually where a river enters an ocean.

Eutrophication. Chemical and biological changes that take place after a lake, estuary, or stream receives nutrients from nitrates and phosphates from erosion and runoff.

Fertilizer. Substance used to encourage plant growth. Can be man-made chemicals or naturally produced as in the case of manure or compost.

Graywater. Water that has been used for showering, clothes washing, and faucet uses.

Greenhouse effect. The warming of the earth's atmosphere caused by a buildup of carbon dioxide or other trace gases; it is believed by many scientists that this buildup allows light from the sun's rays to heat the earth but prevents a counterbalancing loss of heat.

Hydrogen. An element found naturally in the environment. Water is two parts hydrogen and one part oxygen.

Indicator species. Species that serve as early warnings that a community or an ecosystem is being degraded.

Marsh. A treeless wetland that is dominated by grasses.

Microorganism. A living organism too small to be seen with the naked eye.

National Marine Fisheries Service (NMFS). Also known as NOAA Fisheries, a federal agency responsible for the stewardship of marine ecosystems. NMFS is a division of the Department of Commerce.

Nitrates. Forms of nitrogen used in fertilizer. An overabundant runoff of nitrates accelerates eutrophication.

Nitrogen. An element that in any of its forms (organic, ammonia, nitrate) is great for promoting plant growth. Commonly found in fertilizers and is present in all living things as well as the atmosphere.

Nonpoint source pollution. Pollution discharged over a wide land area, not from one specific location, which enters air or water bodies. Occurs when the rate of materials entering waters exceeds natural levels.

Nonrenewable resource. Resource that is not replaced by natural processes or for which the rate of replacement is much slower than its rate of use.

Organic farming. Method of producing crops and livestock naturally by using organic fertilizer, crop rotation, and natural pest control instead of synthetic pesticides and herbicides.

Oxygen. An element found naturally in the environment including air and water.

Pesticides. Chemicals used to kill insects.

Phosphorus. An element that encourages growth and is commonly found in fertilizers in small amounts.

Phytoremediation. Process of using plants that absorb or neutralize pollutants from soil or water.

Potable Water. Water fit for human consumption.

Precipitation. The return of water to the earth's surface in the form of rain, snow, ice pellets, and hail.

Recharge. The addition of water into a groundwater system.

River basin. The area drained by a river and its tributaries.

Runoff. Rainfall that can't be absorbed into the ground that runs to storm drains or natural water bodies.

Storm drain. Man-made drains that send water runoff to rivers, oceans, lakes, and streams.

Swamp. A wetland dominated by shrubs or trees.

Tides. The rise and fall of the surface of oceans, seas, bays, rivers, and other water bodies caused by the gravitational attraction of the moon and sun occurring unequally on different parts of the earth.

Toxic materials. Any liquid, gaseous, or solid substance(s) in a concentration that, when applied to, discharged to, or deposited in water, may exert a poisonous effect detrimental to man or aquatic life.

Turbidity. Cloudiness caused by the presence of suspended colloids in water; an indicator of water quality.

Upwelling region. Area adjacent to a continent where ocean bottom waters rich in nutrients are brought to the surface.

Wastewater. Water that carries wastes from homes, businesses, and industries; a mixture of water and dissolved or suspended solids.

Wastewater treatment. The processing of wastewater for the removal or reduction of contained solids or other undesirable constituents.

Water cycle (hydrologic cycle). The endless cycle of all the earth's water going through the stages of evaporation, condensation, and precipitation.

Watershed. A geographic area defined by where precipitation drains to a common water body such as a lake or ocean.

Water table. The upper surface of the zone of saturation in which all available pores in the soil and rock in the earth's crust are filled with water.

Xeriscape. Creative landscaping for water and energy efficiency and lower maintenance.

Yield. The quantity of water, expressed either as a continuous rate of flow or as a volume per unit time, which can be collected for a given use, or uses, from surface or groundwater sources in a watershed.

Resources

Books

Borland, Hal. *Sundial of the Seasons*. Philadelphia: Lippincott, 1964.

Bowden, Charles. *Killing the Hidden Waters*. Austin, TX: University of Texas Press, 1977.

Brown, Lester A., Michael Renner, and Brian Halweil. *Vital Signs*. New York: W.W. Norton and Co, 1999.

Clark, Robin, and Janet King. *The Water Atlas: A Unique Visual Analysis of the World's Most Critical Resource*. New York: The New Press, 2004.

De Villiers, Marq. *Water: The Fate of Our Most Precious Resource*. Boston: Houghton Mifflin, 2000.

Gilpin, Laura. *The Rio Grande: River of Destiny*. New York: Duell, Sloan and Pearce, 1949.

Harlowe, Rosie, and Sally Morgan. *Pollution and Waste: Environmental Facts and Experiments*. New York: Kingfisher, 2001.

Harms, Valerie et al. *National Audubon Society Almanac of the Environment*. New York: Putnum, 1994.

Hughes, Langston. "April Rain Song." *The Collected Works of Langston Hughes*. Edited by Arnold Rampersad. Columbia: University of Missouri Press, 2001.

Junger, Sebastian. *The Perfect Storm*. New York: W.W. Norton, 1998.

Miller, Morris. *Debt and Environment: Converging Crisis*. United Nations, 1991.

National Wildlife Federation. *Pollution Problems and Solutions*. New York: Learning Triangle Press, 1998.

Reisner, Marc. *Cadillac Desert*. New York: Viking Penguin, 1986.

Roddick, Anita. *Troubled Water: Saints, Sinners, Truths, and Lies About the Global Water Crisis*. West Sussex: Anita Roddick Publications Ltd., 2004.

Steingraber, Sandra. *Having Faith: An Ecologist's Journey to Motherhood*. Cambridge, MA: Perseus Publishing, 2001.

Swanson, Peter. *Water: The Drop of Life (A Companion to the Public Television Series)*. Minnetonka, MI: Northword Press, 2001.

Vigil, Kenneth. *Clean Water: An Introduction to Water Quality and Water Pollution Control.* Corvallis, OR: Oregon State University Press, 2003.

Zwick, David, and Marcy Benstock. *Water Wasteland: Ralph Nader's Study Group on Water Pollution.* New York: Grossman Publishers, 1971.

Periodicals and Reports

Allen, Scott. "Hurricanes More Powerful, Study Says." *Boston Globe.* August 1, 2005.

American Rivers Campaign. *Dam Removal Success Stories: Restoring Rivers Through Selective Removal of Dams That Don't Make Sense.* Report. Washington, D.C., December 1999.

Barber, Charles, Victor Pratt and R. Vaughan. "Poison and Profits: Cyanide Fishing in the Indo-Pacific." *Environment Magazine,* October 1, 1998.

Borenstein, Seth. "The Melting Tip of the Iceberg." *St. Paul Pioneer Press,* August 3, 2003.

Boston Globe. "Researchers Hope to Unlock Mysteries of the Jellyfish," February 9, 2003.

Chambers, Catherine M., Paul E. Chambers, and John C. Whitehead. "Environmental Preservation and Corporate Involvement: Green Products and Debt-for-Nature Swaps. (Symposium: Socially Responsible Business)." *Review of Business,* June 22, 1993.

Clement, Douglas. "Dam It All." *Fedgazette,* September 2001.

Department for International Development (DFID) of the UK Government under the Knowledge and Research (KAR) Programme. "Handbook for the Assessment of Catchment Water Demand and Use." May 2003.

DiChristina, Mariette. "Sea Power." *Popular Science.* June 1, 1995.

Egan, Timothy. "Grass Is Gone on Other Side of These Fences." *New York Times,* May 5, 2001.

Egan, Timothy. "Near Vast Bodies of Water, Land Lies Parched." *New York Times,* May 5, 2001.

Environmental News Network. "U.S. Economy Depends on Clean Water," news release, August 12, 2001.

Environment News Service. "Hurricane Activity Accelerates in U.S. Long Term Forecast," news release, July 23, 2001.

Environment News Service. "International Team Combats Black Sea Decline," news release, October 10, 2001.

Environment News Service. "Lake Victoria Battles Biodiversity Breakdown," news release, December 1, 2000.

Environmental News Service. "The United Nations Committee on Economic, Cultural, and Social Rights," news release, November 27, 2002.

Environmental Protection Agency Water Quality Inventory, 2000 Report.

E-wire. "Nation's Most Senior River Activist Declares Colorado Most Endangered Watershed," news release, April 7, 2000.

Food and Agriculture Organization of the United Nations (FAO). *The State of World Fisheries and Aquaculture, 1996.* Report. Rome, 1997.

Graham, Wade. "Houseboat Heaven: Flush It." Editorial, *Los Angeles Times.* June 19, 2005.

Hall, Landon. "Agency Sued Over Putting Hydropower Ahead of Fish." Associated Press, *Seattle Post-Intelligencer.* May 4, 2001.

Hayden, Thomas, and Megan Barnett. "Bigger, Badder Tropical Blows." *U.S. News & World Report.* September 12, 2005.

Holmes, B. "Blue Revolutionaries." *New Scientist,* July 12, 1996.

Hotz, Robert Lee, and Kenneth Reich. "Aquifer Levels May Lift, Lower L.A. Land." *Los Angeles Times*, August 23, 2001.

Jehl, Douglas. "In Race to Tap the Euphrates, the Upper Hand Is Upstream." *New York Times*, August 25, 2002.

Kay, Jane. "Drinking Water in Peril: MTBE Contaminates 48 Wells in Public System," *San Francisco Chronicle*, August 26, 2001.

Kennedy, Robert F., Jr. "Free Range at Last, Free Range at Last." *Grist Magazine,* November 20, 2000.

Larson, Janet. "Dead Zones Increasing in World's Coastal Waters." Eco-Economy Updates, Earth Policy Institute. June 16, 2004.

Lavelle, Marianne, Joshua Kurlantzick, and David D'Addio. "The Coming Water Crisis." *U.S. News & World Report,* August 12, 2002.

Louma, John. "Water Thieves." *Ecologist,* March 2004.

Lurie, Jon. "A Thirsty World Eyes the Great Lakes." *Circle,* March 31, 2000.

Mann, Michael E., and Philip D. Jones. "Global Surface Temperatures Over the Past Two Millennia." *Journal of Geophysics* 30, no. 15 (2003).

Mazur, Laurie Ann. "Marketing Madness—Excessive Advertising Creates a Consumerist Culture." *E Magazine,* May 15, 1996.

McAllister, D.E., J. Baquero, G. Spiller, and R. Campbell. "A Global Trawling Ground Survey." Unpublished paper prepared for the World Resources Institute, Washington, D.C., 1999.

McKibben, Bill. "Taking the Pulse of the Planet." *Audubon Magazine,* November-December 1999.

Miller, Allen. "Waters of the World." Editorial. *Capital Times,* October 16, 2002.

Montaigne, Fen. "Water Pressure." *National Geographic Magazine,* September 2002.

Moore, Charles. "Trashed." *Natural History* 112, no.9 (2003).

Nation (Thailand). "Water Crisis: Left High and Dry." April 7, 2004.

National Geographic, September 2004, 13.

Naylor, R., R. Goldburg, J. Primavera, N. Kautsky, M. Beveridge, J. Clay, C. Folke, J. Lubchenco, H. Mooney, and M. Troll. "Effect of Aquaculture on World Fish Supplies." *Nature* 405 (2000): 1017–1024.

Nortey, Sam, Jr. "In Africa, a Search for Homemade Solutions." *International Herald Tribune*, August 20, 2005.

Oklahoma Department of Environmental Quality. *Use Less Stuff Newsletter.* November 15, 2001.

Oweyegha-Afundaduula, F. C. "Environment Literacy for Sustainable Development in Africa." Paper presented at the First Conference on Ecology and Sustainable Natural Resource Management, Uganda Institute of Ecology, Queen Elizabeth National Park, Lake Katwe, Uganda. November 1995.

Paengnoy, Anan. "Water Strife Claims Two." *Nation (Thailand).* March 10, 1999.

Panetta, Leon E. (Chair). *America's Living Oceans: Charting a Course for Sea Change.* Pew Oceans Commission Report to Congress. July 2003.

Partners for Environmental Progress. ULS Reports. Ann Arbor, Michigan, 2000.

Pew Oceans Commission. Report to Congress. Executive Summary. May 2003.

Population Reports. "Solutions for a Water-Short World." September 1, 1998.

Postel, Sandra. "Global Water Policy Project." *Grist Magazine,* April 26, 2004.

PR Newswire. "South African Students Win Stockholm Junior Water Prize," news release, August 23, 2005.

Revkin, Andrew C. "FDA Considers New Tests for Environmental Effects." *New York Times*, March 14, 2002.

Rorabaugh, Jim, and Ray Bransfield. "Lands of Contrast, Diversity, and Beauty." *Endangered Species Bulletin,* March-June 2002.

Sample, Ian. "Not Just Warmer: It's the Hottest for 2,000 Years." *Guardian,* September 1, 2003.

Schindler, David W. "The Mysterious Missing Sink." *Nature* 398 (1999): 105-106.

Schoenberger, Karl. "California's E-Waste Recycling Program Hits Stride." *San Jose Mercury News*, July 19, 2005.

Seattle Times. "Seattle-Area Cleaners Spot Need to Switch to Environmentally Friendly Methods." February 17, 2004.

Sevin, Josh. "Water, Water Everywhere," *Grist Magazine*, December 20, 1999.

Sierra Club. *Permitting Disaster in America: How Reforming "Rubber Stamp" Wetland Destruction Permits Will Protect Your Family from More Flood Risks.* Report. 2002.

Sierra Club. *Regional Conservation Committee 2001 Colorado River Report,* http://www.sierraclub.org/rcc/southwest/COreport/.

Smith, Donal. "When Green Earth Turns into Sand." *National Geographic Magazine,* December 2000.

Stiffler, Lisa. "Pesticides Enter Salmon Picture—Lawsuit Claims Toxins Impair Ability of Fish to Smell." *Seattle Post-Intelligencer,* January 31, 2001.

Theriault, Carmen. "Plants That Heal the Earth." *American Gardener,* November-December 2002: 23-27.

Toronto Globe and Mail, "Will Foreigners Drink Canada Dry?" Editorial. May 23, 1998.

Uehling, Mark D. "Free Drugs From Your Faucet," *Salon.* www.salon.com. October 25, 2001.

United Nations Millennium Goals Development Report, 2000.

USA Today Magazine. "Disappearing Lakes, Shrinking Seas." June 2005.

Vivian, John. "Growing Wild: Take Your Home Place (Almost) All the Way Back to Nature (Home Landscaping Part 1)." *Mother Earth News,* December 1, 1997.

Walsh, Edward. "Reagan's First Hill Showdown Already Brewing." *Washington Post,* January 9, 1987.

Washington State Department of Ecology. "Pooping Pets Pose Pollution Predicament," news release, February 4, 2004.

Weiss, Rick. "Key Ocean Fish Species Ravaged, Study Finds." *Washington Post,* May 15, 2003.

Whiteman, Lily. "The Blobs of Summer." *OnEarth Magazine,* Summer 2002: 2.

Work Health Organization, 2001 World Water Development Report.

General Sources

ACNielsen International Research, December 2004.

Gartner Research.

Intergovernmental Panel on Climate Change 2001.

Journey North Teacher's Manual.

Raftelis Financial Consulting. *2002 Water and Wastewater Rate Survey,* U.S. News research.

World Resources 2000-2001, World Resources Institute.

Speeches

Barlow, Maude. "Blue Gold: The Fight to Stop the Corporate Theft of the World's Water." Speech for the Carnegie Council on Ethics and International Affairs Books for Breakfast Program. Online Transcript. December 12, 2002, http://www.carnegiecouncil.org/viewMedia.php/prmID/830.

Bush, George H. W. Speech at Grand Teton National Park, Wyoming, June 13, 1989.

Douglas, Justice William O. Dissenting Opinion. Supreme Court of the United States, No. 70-34, *Sierra Club v. Morton,* 1972.

Johnson, Lyndon B. "To Renew a Nation." Special Message to Congress. March 8, 1968.

Johnson, Lyndon B. "Letter to the President of the Senate and to the Speaker of the House Transmitting an Assessment of the Nation's Water Resources." November 18, 1968.

Television

"China, U.N. Challenged Over Fish," MSNBC.com. Online transcript. November 28, 2001.

"Global Water Supply Central Issue at Stockholm Conference." Reuters News Service. Reported by CNN.com. August 14, 2000.

"Water Arithmetic 'Doesn't Add Up.'" BBC News. Online transcript. March 13, 2000. http://news.bbc.co.uk/1/hi/sci/tech/671800.stm.

"Water Fight." *The NewsHour with Jim Lehrer.* PBS. OnlineTranscript. December 31, 2002. http://www.pbs.org/newshour/bb/environment/july-dec02/water_fight_12-31.html.

Web Sites

Abundant Earth Online. http://www.abundantearth.com.

Earth 911. http://www.earth911.org/master.asp.

Earth Friendly Products. http://www.ecos.com/index.html.

Earth Day Web Site. The Wilderness Society. http://earthday.wilderness.org/.

Earth Save. "A New Global Warming Strategy." http://www.earthsave.org/global-warming.htm.

Environment Canada. Canada Department of the Environment. http://www.ec.gc.ca/water.

Environmental Protection Agency. http://www.epa.gov.

Global Response Web Site. http://www.globalresponse.org/.

Global Rivers Environmental Education Network. http://www.green.org/.

Green Earth Cleaning. http://www.greenearthcleaning.com.

Green Team Tips—National Zoo. http://j.cfmx.si.edu/Publications/GreenTeam/.

Grist Magazine Online. http://www.grist.org.

Heifer International. http://www.heifer.org.

International Carwash Association. http://www.carlove.org.

Marine Aquarium Council. http://www.aquariumcouncil.org.

NASA. http://earthobservatory.nasa.gov/.

National Renewable Energy Laboratory Web Site. http://www.nrel.gov.

National Resources Defense Council. http://www.nrdc.org.

Polluted Runoff (Nonpoint Source Pollution) 2005. U.S. Environmental Protection Agency. http://www.epa.gov/owow/nps/.

San Diego Earth Times. http://www.sdearthtimes.com.

Seafood Watch Online. Monterey Bay Aquarium. http://www.Seafoodwatch.org.

Sierra Club. http://www.sierraclub.org.

Surf Your Watershed. Environmental Protection Agency. http://www.epa.gov/surf/.

SVTC 2004 Report / National Safety Council. http://www.svtc.org/cleancc/pubs/poisonpc2004.htm.

United Nations Environmental Programme. Climate Change Information Sheet 13. Information Unit for Conventions. http://www.thewaterpage.com/climatech_fact_sheet13.htm.

United States Senate. http://www.senate.gov/general/contact_information/senators_cfm.cfm.

U.S. Army Corps of Engineers, FEMA. www.usace.army.mil/inet/functions/cw.

Waste Reduction. Oklahoma Department of Environmental Quality. http://www.deq.state.ok.us/mainlinks/uls/conservationtips/waste.htm.

Water, Environment, Sanitation. WHO / UNICEF. http://www.unicef.org/wes/.

The Water Page. http://www.thewaterpage.com/aral.htm.

The World. http://www.theworld.org/worldfeature/edpick/pump.shtml.

WaterKeeper Alliance. www.waterkeeper.org.

About the Wyland Foundation

The Wyland Foundation is a 501c3 nonprofit organization that inspires people to care about our oceans and related marine ecosystems. Founded in 1993 by marine life artist Wyland, the foundation encourages involvement in conservation through classroom education programs, community service, and art in public places. In the last thirteen years, the foundation has been responsible for more than ninety-three conservation-themed marine life murals in seventy cities in twelve countries around the world, and has staged marine resources education and science tours in every state in the nation, including a fifteen-state East Coast cleanup tour during summer 2004. Subsequent tours are slated for selected regions of the United States and around the world for the next five years.

Other foundation-initiated projects include the Wyland Ocean Challenge, "Clean Water for the 21st Century . . . and Beyond," a nationwide art and science educational curriculum in partnership with the Scripps Institution of Oceanography (UCSD). The program was created to foster a sense of environmental responsibility in the next generation, and is available free to every school in America, grades K-12. The curriculum uses online technology, case studies, and creative exploration of water through digital video, field experiments, research papers, and art to explore how students can protect our planet's oceans, rivers, lakes, streams, and wetlands. Other foundation involvements include the California Coastal Commission License Plate program, the Pediatric Cancer Research Foundation Holiday Card program, and the Orange County March of Dimes. The foundation supports up to one hundred conservation, scientific research, and education groups every year, and takes part in up to twenty-five conservation-themed public events each year.

For more information, visit http://www.wylandoceanchallenge.org or http://www.wylandfoundation.org

About the Authors

Wyland

One of the world's most recognizable artists, Wyland has developed an international reputation for his commitment to marine life conservation, most notably his monumental marine life murals, the Whaling Walls. Spanning thousands of square feet, these massive works of art expose more than one billion people each year to the thrilling diversity and beauty of life that exists below the surface of our ocean planet.

Today, this multifaceted artist works in multiple mediums, including oils, watercolors, acrylics, Japanese ink paintings, bronze sculptures, fine art photography, and mixed media. He is considered one of the most successful working artists today, with galleries throughout the United States, and more than half a million collectors around the world.

Perhaps most important, his nonprofit Wyland foundation, in partnership with the Scripps Institution of Oceanography, is actively engaged in alerting millions of students around the world to become caring, informed stewards of our oceans, rivers, lakes, streams, and wetlands.

Steve Creech

Steve Creech serves as educational project director for the nonprofit Wyland Foundation. A former newspaper reporter and children's book author, he is coauthor of *Chicken Soup for the Ocean Lover's Soul*. His articles have appeared in such newspapers as the *Orange County Register, Pasadena Star News,* and *Anaheim Bulletin,* and magazines such as *Skin Diver, Sport Diver, React for Kids,* and *Elan*, and literary publications including the *Orange Coast Review*. You can write to him at the Wyland Foundation, 2171 Laguna Canyon Road, Laguna Beach, CA 92651.

Sue Ann Balogh

Sue Ann Balogh is director of education for the nonprofit Wyland Foundation. She holds a master's degree in education from Cal State University–San Diego and is currently developing environmentally themed science and conservation education programs, including the Wyland Ocean Challenge, "Clean Water for the 21st Century . . . and Beyond," a free classroom program for schools throughout the nation in partnership with the Scripps Institution of Oceanography (UCSD).